Paris

by Elisabeth Morris

Elisabeth Morris was born and grew up in
France. She studied languages in London
where she settled, contributing to various
educational publications and eventually
turning to travel writing. Since returning to
France with her family, she has written a
number of guide books for several British
and French publishers, including the AA's
European Regional Guide Brittany and
AA/Thomas Cook Travellers Paris, and
contributed to many more. She enjoys
discovering new horizons and has travelled
throughout Europe to the wilderness of the
Arctic regions and across North Africa.

Above: lanterns against the façade of Notre-Dame

AA Publishing

A French breakfast

Written by Elisabeth Morris.

First published 1998. Reprinted Jun and Nov 1998; Mar, May and Aug 1999.
Second edition Jan 2000. Reprinted Apr 2001.
Reprinted Apr 2002. Information verified and updated.
Reprinted Jun 2003.
Reprinted 2004 with amendments.
Reprinted Apr 2004.
Reprinted 2005. Information verified and updated.
Reprinted May, Aug, Oct and Nov 2005.

© Automobile Association Developments Limited 2004

Published by AA Publishing, a trading name of Automobile Association Developments Limited, whose registered office is Fanum House, Basing View, Basingstoke, Hampshire, RG21 4EA. Registered number 1878835.

Automobile Association Developments Limited retains the copyright in the original edition © 1998 and in all subsequent editions, reprints and amendments.

A CIP catalogue record for this book is available from the British Library.

A02865

Colour separation: BTB Digital Imaging Ltd, Whitchurch, Hampshire
Printed and bound in Italy by Printer Trento S.r.l.

Find out more about AA Publishing and the wide range of travel publications and services the AA provides by visiting our website at www.theAA.com/bookshop

Contents

About this Book

This book is divided into five sections to cover the most important aspects of your visit to Paris.

Viewing Paris pages 5–14
An introduction to Paris by the author
Paris's Features
Essence of Paris
The Shaping of Paris
Peace and Quiet
Paris's Famous

Top Ten pages 15–26
The author's choice of the Top Ten places to see in Paris, each with practical information.

What to See pages 27–90
Two sections: Paris and Ile de France, each with its own brief introduction and an alphabetical listing of the main attractions
Practical information
Snippets of 'Did You Know…' information
4 suggested walks
3 suggested tours
2 features

Where To… pages 91–116
Detailed listings of the best places to eat, stay, shop, take the children and be entertained.

Practical Matters pages 117–24
A highly visual section containing essential travel information.

Maps
All map references are to the individual maps found in the What to See section of this guide.
For example, Notre-Dame has the reference
✚ 29E2 – indicating the page on which the map is located and the grid square in which the cathedral is to be found. A list of the maps that have been used in this travel guide can be found in the index.

Prices
Where appropriate, an indication of the cost of an establishment is given by € signs:
€€€ denotes higher prices, €€ denotes average prices, while € denotes lower charges.

Star Ratings
Most of the places described in this book have been given a separate rating:
✪✪✪ Do not miss
✪✪ Highly recommended
✪ Worth seeing

Viewing
Paris

Above: *a café in the Saint-Germain district*

5

Elisabeth Morris's Paris

'Villages' such as St-Germain-des-Prés (above) and the conviviality of café life (below) are just part of Paris's charm

Paris never leaves me indifferent. It has the power to rouse strong feelings in me, whatever mood I am in: admiration, exhilaration, irritation and even frustration, but above all fascination as time and again I am bewitched by its charm and diversity.

Paris may seem straightforward and orderly to the first-time visitor as it unfolds its wealth of stately monuments, but it is in fact a complex city and its beauty has many facets; besides the vast open vistas there are picturesque villages like Saint-Germain-des-Prés, Le 'Marais or Montmartre where you may suddenly come across a tiny square steeped in a romantic old-world atmosphere or be confronted with a bold modern sculpture defiantly competing with a medieval master-piece. What never ceases to amaze me, however, is the overall sense of harmony that pervades these contrasting features and confers on the city a unique homogeneity.

Paris is a melting-pot of new, daring, even outrageous ideas in the fields of art, fashion, architecture, cuisine, lifestyle, politics and sociology. Living in the midst of this continuous creative outburst is tremendously stimulating, but I also enjoy standing back and relaxing at lunchtime in the peaceful Jardins du Palais-Royal, at the heart of the city, or taking a stroll along the river at sunset when Parisians set aside their hurried daily pursuit of an elusive happiness and unashamedly give in to their inclination for enjoyment. Paris then seems more alive and exciting than ever.

Bistros and Cafés
You may think that *bistro* is just another name for *café* but there is a subtle difference. Cafés were traditionally the haunt of fashionable society and artists. Bistros are cafés of modest appearance where locals meet regularly for a drink, a game of dice and sometimes a snack. The number of cafés and bistros has decreased considerably in recent years.

6

Paris's Features

Geography
• Situated at the heart of northern France, some 250km from the sea, Paris lies on the banks of the meandering River Seine.

The City
• The city is small and compact, entirely surrounded by the boulevard périphérique, a congested 35km-long dual carriageway. Green spaces cover an area of 366ha excluding the Bois de Boulogne and Bois de Vincennes and there is one tree for every four Parisians.

Greater Paris
• The surrounding area, known as the *banlieue*, includes densely populated suburbs, dormitory towns and traditional villages scattered through the green belt, as well as several new towns. The whole region enjoys a reasonably dry climate, fairly cold in winter, hot and sunny in summer.

An unmistakeable skyline – the Tour Eiffel beyond the pont Neuf

Administration
• Paris is a municipality administered by a council and a mayor like any other town in France, but it is also a *département* (county) headed by a *préfet*.
• Paris is divided into 20 *arrondissements* numbered from 1 to 20 starting from the Louvre in the historic centre.

Population
• The city has just over 2 million inhabitants but nearly 11 million people, almost one-fifth of the French population, live in Greater Paris.

The Oldest...
• The oldest bridge is the pont Neuf (New Bridge!) dating from 1578.
• The oldest church is St-Germain-des-Prés, built in the 11th century.
• The oldest houses date from the 15th century; the Musée de Cluny is one of them (▶ 62).
• The oldest tree, planted in 1601, stands in the square Viviani, on the Left Bank opposite Notre-Dame.

Paris's Highest Monuments
Tour Eiffel: 317m
Tour Montparnasse: 209m
Grande Arche de la Défense: 110m
Dôme des Invalides: 105m
Panthéon: 83m
Sacré-Coeur: 80m`
Notre-Dame: 69m
Arc de Triomphe: 50m

Paris to...by Road
Amsterdam: 504km
Berlin: 1,069km
Brussels: 308km
Geneva: 538km
London: 343km
Luxembourg: 376km
Madrid: 1,310km
Rome: 1,417km

7

Essence of Paris

Paris is order, harmony, beauty and elegance...the result of bold town planning that was particularly successful in marrying tradition and innovation, sometimes with stunning effects, as in the case of the stark glass pyramid erected in front of the Louvre.

Paris is also passion, youthful energy and a stimulating cultural life.

But Paris is above all the capital of good living: the best of French cuisine, an enticing choice of gastronomic specialities from various countries, the glamorous world of *haute couture* and eccentric fashion, and a sparkling nightlife.

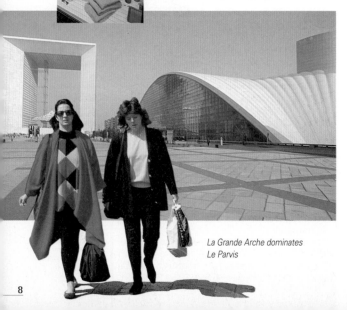

La Grande Arche dominates Le Parvis

THE 10 ESSENTIALS

If you have only a short time to visit Paris and would like to take home unforgettable memories, here are the essentials:

• **Take a boat trip along the Seine** from the pont de l'Alma and admire the stately monuments (➤ 22, 24, 41 and 43) whose splendour is dramatically enhanced at night by powerful spotlights.

• **Climb to the top of the Tour Eiffel** for an aerial view of Paris (➤ 25); guaranteed thrill from the panoramic lift.

• **Take a morning walk through the Jardin du Luxembourg** and stand beside the romantic Fontaine de Médicis (➤ 12).

• **Sit outside Les Deux Magots Café** in boulevard St-Germain, on the Left Bank, and watch the world go by. Street bustle peaks around lunchtime and from 6PM (➤ 71).

• **Stand on the pont de la Tournelle** near Notre Dame: look downriver for panoramic views of 'old Paris' (Ile de la Cité and beyond) and upriver for contrasting views of 'new Paris' (Bercy and Institut du Monde Arabe, ➤ 54).

• **Stroll along the quais** and browse through the *bouquinistes*' stock of old prints and books (➤ 24).

• **Take the funicular to Sacré Coeur** at the top of Montmartre for stunning views of the city (➤ 70).

• **Go to the colourful Moulin-Rouge** show and discover the glamour of traditional Parisian entertainment (➤ 58).

• **Stand on the place de la Concorde** at night and look up the Champs-Elysées. The illuminated avenue, gently rising towards the Arc de Triomphe, offers one of the most perfect urban vistas in the world (➤ 17).

• **Mingle with Parisians** doing their daily shopping in street markets along the rue Mouffetard (Quartier Latin), or on Sundays, buying organic food on boulevard Raspail.

A trip along the Seine is an ideal way to see many of the city's sights

Place de la Concorde, the great square at one end of the Champs-Elysées

The Shaping of Paris

c250 BC
A Celtic tribe, called the Parisii, settles on the Ile de la Cité.

52 BC
The Parisii are defeated by the Romans.

2nd century AD
Building of the Gallo-Roman city of Lutetia.

c300
Lutetia is renamed Paris.

508
Clovis, king of the Franks, chooses Paris as his capital.

845
First Viking raid on Paris.

c1100
Abélard teaches in Paris and meets Héloïse. The Quartier Latin spreads to the left bank.

1163–1245
Building of Notre-Dame Cathedral.

1215
Foundation of the Paris University.

c1220
The Royal Palace of Le Louvre is completed.

1358
The merchants of Paris, headed by Etienne Marcel, rebel against royal authority and call for tax reforms.

1408
During the Hundred Years' War, Paris is occupied by the English.

1431
King Henry VI of England is crowned king of France in Notre-Dame.

1437
Charles VII liberates Paris.

c1470
The first printing-press is set up in the Sorbonne.

1559
Foundation of the French Reformed Church.

1594
King Henri IV enters Paris, cheered by the population, and thus puts an end to the Wars of Religion.

1570–1610
The Louvre is extended.

Napoleon I dressed in his coronation robes

1605
The building of the place Royale (now place des Vosges), Paris's oldest square, leads to the development of the Marais district.

1660–70
The Louvre is extended once more.

c1670
The first cafés become popular.

1680
Foundation of the Comédie-Française, France's most prestigious theatre. Louis XIV leaves Paris for Versailles.

1755–75
Building of the place Louis XV (now place de la Concorde).

1783
First-ever balloon flight by Pilâtre de Rozier.

1789
The fall of the Bastille marks the beginning of the French Revolution.

1804
Napoleon is crowned emperor in Notre-Dame Cathedral.

1816
Gas lighting is installed in the city. The first steamships sail along the Seine.

General Eisenhower in liberated Paris, 1944

1852–70
Baron Haussmann reshapes Paris.

1870
Paris is besieged by the Prussians and is forced to capitulate. The Hôtel de Ville is burnt down and is rebuilt in under 10 years.

1889
The Tour Eiffel is the main attraction at the World Fair.

1900
The first métro line is inaugurated.

1914
Paris is saved from German occupation by the Battle of the Marne.

1919
Inauguration of the world's first commercial airline between Paris and London.

1940
Paris is occupied by German troops.

1944
Paris is liberated.

1947
First-ever fashion parade, organised by Christian Dior.

1968
Series of student demonstrations followed by a general strike.

1973
The boulevard périphérique is completed.

1977
The office of Mayor is reinstated after 100 years; Jacques Chirac is elected. Centre Georges Pompidou is inaugurated.

1986
Inauguration of the Musée d'Orsay.

1989
The Grand Louvre, the Opéra-Bastille and the Grande Arche de la Défense are inaugurated for the bicentenary of the Revolution.

1996
Opening of the new Bibliothèque Nationale.

1998
The football World Cup final takes place in the newly built Stade de France in St-Denis – and is won by France.

2000
The Eiffel Tower is revamped with glittering halogen lighting.

2002
Euro notes and coins introduced.

Peace & Quiet

Paris is a compact, densely populated city and the pace of life is notoriously hectic. Fortunately, the city has its quiet spots, full of charm and mystery, ideal for relaxing after a head-spinning shopping spree in boulevard Haussmann or a marathon visit to the Louvre.

Paris's green spaces cover an area of about 2,000ha. They come in all shapes and sizes, from the tiny square du Vert Galant on the Ile de la Cité to the imposing Bois de Boulogne on the outskirts of town. Names vary according to size: *squares* are small gardens, often occupying the centre of a square such as the square Louis XIII in the place des Vosges; *jardins* are larger and usually formal in design, such as the Jardin des Tuileries; *parcs* are freer in style: they can be romantic like the parc Monceau or futuristic like the parc André Citroën. Whether you wish to take a brief pause or are longing for a day away from it all, you should find what you are looking for in the selection below.

Jardin du Luxembourg, popular with students as a retreat from the nearby Sorbonne

In the City Centre

Square du Vert Galant – this triangular green patch, situated at the western end of the Ile de la Cité, offers a splendid view of the Louvre.

Arènes de Lutèce – surrounded by greenery, the ruins of the city's Gallo-Roman amphitheatre form a picturesque setting at the heart of the busy Quartier Latin.

Square Viviani – adjacent to the small medieval church of St-Julien-le-Pauvre, on the Left Bank, it shelters Paris's oldest tree. Admire the delightful view of Notre-Dame.

Jardin du Luxembourg – situated a stone's throw from the Sorbonne, this attractive French-style garden is traditionally the favourite haunt of students and lovers, who particularly favour the area surrounding the Fontaine de Médicis, named after Marie de Médicis, who commissioned the Palais du Luxembourg (now the Senate) and the gardens.

Jardin du Palais-Royal – walking under the arches into the garden is like taking a journey back in time: the noise of traffic fades away and the visual impression is one of 18th-century elegance and harmony.

Parc Monceau – this English-style park is scattered with 18th-century follies. Combine a quiet stroll here with a visit to the nearby Musée Nissim de Camondo (➤ 63) and Musée Cernuschi (➤ 39).

Further Out

Parc des Buttes-Chaumont – complete with lake, rocky island, bridges and waterfall, this was the first park to be laid out in the city's northern districts.

Parc André-Citroën – this ultra-modern park in the 15th *arrondissement* combines architecture with nature and experiments with colours, metals and water to create different impressions and striking contrasts.

Bois de Boulogne and Bois de Vincennes – landscaped in the English style at the end of the 19th century with artificial lakes, lawns, woodland areas, footpaths and tracks for horse-riding and bicycling, these offer an ideal one-day break from city life. The Bois de Boulogne boasts two racecourses as well as cafés and restaurants while the Bois de Vincennes has a racecourse, a zoo and a working farm open to the public.

Top: *Bois de Vincennes, an extensive area of parkland on the edge of the city*
Above: *floating wooden boats in the Jardin des Tuileries, a popular pastime with Parisian children*

13

Paris's Famous

Molière

The son of an upholsterer established near Les Halles, Molière turned down a promising career in law to become an actor. His first attempts at directing his own company ended in disaster and...prison! However he persevered and success finally came in 1659 with *Les Précieuses ridicules*, the first of many incisive comedies in which he satirised human nature in general and French society in particular. He worked and lived near the Palais-Royal, where the Comédie-Française is now established; the armchair in which Molière was playing the rôle of the *Malade imaginaire* when he collapsed and died in 1673, is inside.

André Le Nôtre

André Le Nôtre was Louis XIV's (the Sun King) famous landscape gardener. He conceived his gardens along architectural lines and showed an extraordinary flair for harmonious proportions. He not only designed the magnificent parks of Vaux-le-Vicomte and Versailles, but also left his mark on Paris by redesigning the Jardin des Tuileries and creating the vast vista leading up to the Arc de Triomphe, later to become the Champs-Elysées.

Baron Haussmann

During the second half of the 19th century, Baron Haussmann's brilliant town planning transformed Paris from a squalid medieval town into a spacious, modern city. The Ile de la Cité underwent major surgery, to an extent which seems excessive today, and several wide arteries were opened up along the left and right banks; the place de l'Etoile and its 12 radiating avenues were created, and green spaces were provided all over the town centre.

Geneviève and Attila
Born just outside Paris around AD 420, Geneviève was a devout Christian. In 451, as the Huns were appoaching Paris, panic spread among the people who prepared to leave the city. But Geneviève galvanised them into organising the town's defences, and Attila and his army were forced back. Geneviève later became the patron saint of Paris.

Jacques Chirac

Jacques Chirac was mayor of Paris from 1977 to 1995. During that time, he continued the work of his famous predecessors, including the systematic cleaning of the town's monuments, and the part restoration of the avenue des Champs-Elysées to its former splendour. He resigned as mayor when he was elected president in 1995. In 2002, he was elected to his second term of office.

Top Ten

Above and right: *a fountain and pipes at Centre Georges Pompidou*

1
Centre Georges Pompidou

Not to everyone's taste, but undeniably eye-catching

This spacious and convivial art centre, in the heart of historic Paris, houses under on roof all forms of modern and contemporary art.

www.centrepompidou.fr

 29E3

✉ Place Georges-Pompidou, 75004 Paris

☎ 01 44 78 12 33

🕐 Centre: Wed–Mon. Modern art museum and exhibitions: 11–9. Library: weekdays 12–10; weekends 11–10. Brancusi workshop 2–6

🍴 Restaurant (€€), café and snack bar

🚇 Rambuteau, Hôtel de Ville

🚌 38, 47, 75

♿ Excellent

✋ Free access; museum: moderate (includes Brancusi workshop, children's workshop and level 6)

❓ Audio guides, cash dispenser, shops

With 25,000 visitors a day, the Centre Georges Pompidou is now one of Paris's top sights. Yet at the time it was built, close to the historic Marais which is famous for its elegant architecture, the 'refinery', as Rogers and Piano's post-modern building was nicknamed, deeply shocked French people. In fact, the revolutionary concept of this open-plan 'house of culture for all' ensured its success and brought life back to the district. The centre has had its first major face-lift and been completely refurbished inside; its main asset, the Musée National d'Art Moderne, reached by the external escalator, gained extra exhibition space in the process. The museum is dedicated to the main trends of 20th-century art from 1905 to the present day. Modern art is displayed on level 5. Particularly well represented are Fauvism (Dufy, Derain, Matisse), Cubism (Braque, Picasso, Léger), Dadaism, Surrealism (Dali, Miró), Expressionism (Soutine, Kirchner, Modigliani and to a lesser extent Chagall), various forms of abstract art (Kandinsky, Klee, but also Poliakoff, Dubuffet and the Cobra movement), and pre-1960 American painting. The collections of contemporary art (level 4) include exponents of the new realism (Arman, César), of Pop Art (Warhol), of Minimalist art (Sol Lewitt, Buren) and of monochromes (Manzoni, Klein).

The centre also houses a library, the Institute for Acoustic and Musical Research, the Centre for Industrial Creation, a large exhibition hall, a children's workshop and a reconstruction of Brancusi's workshop.

2
Les Champs-Elysées

For most visitors this prestigious avenue epitomises French elegance, but it is also a dazzling place of entertainment and a luxury shopping mall.

In the late 17th century, Le Nôtre designed a gently rising alleyway as an extension of the Jardin des Tuileries. This later lost its rustic appearance and became a fashionable avenue lined with elegant restaurants and cafés. Nowadays it is the traditional venue for a variety of events such as the Paris Marathon, the arrival of the Tour de France and the march past on 14 July, which celebrates France's national day. But 'les Champs' (the fields) is also a place where people of all ages just relax and feel alive.

The lower section, stretching from the place de la Concorde (with breathtaking views along the whole length of the avenue) to the Rond-Point des Champs-Elysées, is laid out as an English-style park shaded by imposing chestnut trees. On the left are the Grand and Petit Palais, two temples of the arts, while on the right is a monument to the French Resistance hero, Jean Moulin, who was reburied in the Panthéon on 19 December 1964.

The upper section stretches from the Rond-Point, designed by Le Nôtre, to the Arc de Triomphe. This is the 'modern' part of the avenue, with its pavements now revamped and restored to their former comfortable width. Banks, cinemas, airline offices, car showrooms, and large cafés spread out on the pavements, lining the way to the place de l'Etoile. Fashion boutiques cluster along the arcades running between the Champs-Elysées and the parallel rue de Ponthieu. Some shops remain open well into the night and the bustle only quietens down in the early hours of the morning.

www.monum.fr

28B4

Avenue des Champs-Elysées, 75008 Paris

Choice of restaurants (€–€€€)

Concorde, Champs-Elysées-Clemenceau, Franklin-D Roosevelt, George V, Charles-de-Gaulle-Etoile

32, 42, 73

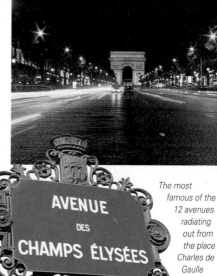

The most famous of the 12 avenues radiating out from the place Charles de Gaulle

3

La Grande Arche de
la Défense

www.grandearche.com

➕ Off map 28A5

✉ 1 parvis de la Défense,
92044 Paris-La Défense

☎ 01 49 07 27 57 (Grande
Arche)

🕐 Grande Arche: daily
10–7

🍴 Rooftop restaurant,
snackbars and cafés in
Les Quatre Temps
shopping centre (€) and
in the CNIT (€ and €€)

Ⓜ La Défense

🚌 73, Balabus in summer

♿ Good

🛗 Lift Grande Arche:
moderate

❓ Video presentation,
guided tours, shops

A striking modern symbol

*Symbolically guarding the western approach to the
city, the Grande Arche is both a recognition of
tradition and a bold step towards the future.*

From the arch's roof top (110m above ground), accessible
by the exterior lift, a marvellous view unfolds in a straight
line along an axis to the Arc de Triomphe and, beyond, to
the Obelisk at place de la Concorde and to the Louvre,
extending the magnificent vista opened up by Le Nôtre.
The arch was inaugurated in 1989 for the bicentenary
celebrations of the French Revolution and is now a major
tourist attraction. The stark simplicity of its architectural
outline and the materials used are definitely contemporary,
while its sheer size is a marvel of modern technology. The
Danish architect, Otto von Spreckelsen, built a perfect
hollow concrete cube covered over with glass and white
Carrara marble. Steps lead up to the central platform,
where the lifts are to be found.

The arch dominates a vast square, known as Le Parvis,
decorated with colourful sculptures, including a red
'stabile' by Calde, and flanked by another remarkable
building: the CNIT (Centre of New Industries and
Technology), shaped like an upside-down-shell, which
serves mainly as a conference centre but is also a pleasant
meeting place for business people. There are several cafés
and a branch of the FNAC, the French equivalent of Virgin
stores, stocking a large selection of CDs covering a wide
spectrum of musical tastes.

Opposite, there is a huge shopping centre known as
Les Quatre Temps, which has some of the best shopping
bargains in Paris. Its focal point is the vast hyper-
market Auchan.

4
Les Invalides

This is one of Paris's most imposing architectural ensembles, built around two churches and housing several museums.

The Hôtel National des Invalides was commissioned by Louis XIV as a home for wounded soldiers. It is a splendid example of 17th-century architecture, the classical austerity of its 200m-long façade being offset by the baroque features of the Eglise du Dôme, with its gilt dome glittering above the slate roofs of the stone buildings. The huge esplanade filling the gap between the river and the monumental entrance enhances the majesty of the building.

The museums are accessible from the arcaded main courtyard. The Musée de l'Armée is one of the richest museums of its kind in the world. It contains weapons from all over the world, armour and uniforms, mementoes of famous generals, paintings, documents and models. Particularly striking is the comprehensive permanent exhibition devoted to the Second World War.

The Musée des Plans-Reliefs is a fascinating collection of models of fortified French towns, originally started at Louis XIV's request.

On the far side of the courtyard is the entrance to St-Louis-des-Invalides, the soldiers' church, which contains a colourful collection of flags brought back from various campaigns; the organ here dates from the 17th century.

The magnificent Eglise du Dôme, built by Jules Hardouin-Mansart, is a striking contrast: an elegant façade with two tiers of Doric and Corinthian columns and an imposing gilt dome surmounted by a slender lantern. The splendid interior decoration is enhanced by the marble floor. The open circular crypt houses Napoleon's red porphyry tomb.

www.invalides.org

⊞ 28B3

✉ Esplanade des Invalides, 75007 Paris

☎ 01 44 42 37 72

🕐 10–5 (6 Apr–Sep). Closed 1 Jan, 1 May, 1 Nov, 25 Dec

🍴 Restaurant (€)

Ⓜ Invalides, La Tour Maubourg, Varenne

🚌 82, 92 ♿ Good

✋ Moderate

❓ Audio-visual shows, guided tours, shops

Eglise du Dôme beyond the Cour d'Honneur and the soldier's church

5
Le Louvre

www.louvre.fr

28C3

99 rue de Rivoli 75001
Paris Cedex 01. Main
entrance via the pyramid

Recorded information: 01
40 20 51 51; reception
desk: 01 40 20 53 17;
visitors with disabilities:
0140 20 59 90

Thu–Sun 9–6, Mon and
Wed 9AM–9.45PM.
Closed 1 Jan, 1 May, 11
Nov and 25 Dec

Palais-Royal/Musée du
Louvre

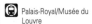
Just one of the 30,000-odd works on show

This former royal palace, which celebrated its bicentenary in 1993, is today one of the largest museums in the world.

The Palace

Excavations carried out in 1977 under the Cour Carrée, the courtyard surrounded by the oldest part of the palace, led to the discovery of the original castle built around 1200 by King Philippe-Auguste, which remained a fortress until it was razed to the ground to make way for a Renaissance palace. The tour of the foundations of this medieval Louvre, including the base of the keep, the moat and the outer wall, starts from the main entrance hall under the glass pyramid.

The first palace, built by Pierre Lescot in the style of the Italian Renaissance, was enlarged round the Cour Carrée and along the Seine during the following 200 years.

It is said that Molière performed in front of the court in the splendid Salle des Cariatides where Greek and Roman antiquities are now displayed. Louis XIV enclosed the Cour Carrée with the stately colonnade that faces the Church of St-Germain-l'Auxerrois. Soon afterwards, however, the King left for Versailles and the palace was neglected by the royal family and the court.

Building was resumed by Napoleon, who built part of the north wing and erected the exquisite Arc de Triomphe du Carrousel. During the second half of the 19th century, Napoleon III completed the Louvre along its rue de Rivoli side.

The Museum

The museum was founded in 1793 to house the royal art collections, which were subsequently enriched to the point that a large part of its vast stock could not be displayed. This prompted President Mitterrand to launch a complete renovation of the buildings and to extend the museum over the whole of the Louvre; the project became known as the 'Grand Louvre'. A huge entrance hall was created under a stunning glass pyramid, designed by Ieoh Ming Peï placed in the centre of the Cour Napoleon. This gives access to three main areas known as Sully, Denon and Richelieu.

The collections are divided into eight departments:

• Egyptian Antiquities include a pink granite *Sphinx from Tanis*, a huge *head of Amenophis IV-Akhenaten* and the famous *Seated Scribe*.

• The most remarkable exhibits in the Oriental Antiquities Department must be the *Assyrian winged bulls*.

• The department of Greek, Etruscan and Roman Antiquities contains numerous masterpieces: do not miss the *Vénus de Milo*, the *Winged Victory* and the Graeco-Roman sculpture in the Salle des Cariatides.

• The painting collections comprise a fine selection from the Italian school (works by Giotto, Fra Angelico, Leonardo da Vinci, Veronese, Titian and Raphael), from the French school (Poussin, Watteau, Georges de la Tour), from the Dutch school (Rembrandt, Rubens and Vermeer) and works by Spanish masters (Murillo, Goya and El Greco).

• French sculpture is particularly well represented and includes fine works by Jean Goujon, Houdon and Pradier.

• *Objets d'art* are now displayed to full advantage in the Richelieu wing; among them are beautiful tapestries and historic items such as Charlemagne's sword.

• The department of Graphic Art, houses drawings, prints and watercolours. The newly created department of Islamic Art will gradually expand over the next few years.
In addition, there is a display of art collections from Africa, Asia, Oceania and the Americas.

The Carrousel du Louvre is a luxury underground shopping precinct with an inverted pyramid in its centre.

Two wildly disparate styles of architecture symbolise the museum's progression into the 20th century

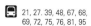 21, 27. 39, 48, 67, 68, 69, 72, 75, 76, 81, 95

Several restaurants (€ and €€) and cafés below the pyramid and in the Carrousel du Louvre

Excellent

Moderate until 3pm, reduced fee after 3 and Sun, free on 1st Sun of the month. To avoid a long wait, buy your ticket in advance: www.louvre.fr

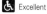 Guided tours, lectures, concerts, film shows, shops. Information: 01 40 20 52 09

6
Notre-Dame

www.cathedraldeparis.com

✚ 29E2

✉ Place du Parvis Notre-Dame, 75004 Paris

☎ 01 42 34 56 10

This masterpiece of Gothic architecture is one of Paris's most famous landmarks and one of France's most visited religious monuments.

In 1163, the Bishop of Paris, Maurice de Sully, launched the building of the cathedral, which took nearly 200 years to complete. One of the architects involved was Pierre de Montreuil, who also built the nearby Sainte-Chapelle (➤ 73). Later alterations deprived the church of its rood screen and of some of its original stained glass; its statues were mutilated during the Revolution because the Commune thought they were likenesses of the kings of France; the cathedral also lost all its original bells, except the 'gros bourdon', known as Emmanuel, which is traditionally heard on occasions of national importance. Restoration work was carried out in the 19th century by the famous architect Viollet-le-Duc and the area round the cathedral was cleared.

From across the vast square in front of the cathedral you can admire the harmonious proportions and almost perfect symmetry of the façade. The richly decorated portals are surmounted by statues of the kings of Judaea restored by Viollet-le-Duc. Above the central rose window, a colonnade links the elegant twin towers; there is a splendid view from the south tower, if you can face up to the 387-step climb.

The nave is 130m long, 48m wide and 35m high; the side chapels are richly decorated with paintings, sculptures and funeral monuments. Note the beautiful rose window at each end of the transept. The former vestry, on the right of the chancel, houses the Cathedral Treasure, which includes a piece of the Holy Cross.

🕐 Cathedral: daily 8–6:45; closed some religious feast days. Treasure: 9:30–11:30 and 1–5:30; closed Sun. Towers: 9:30–7:30 Apr–Sep (9:30–11PM Sat–Sun, Jul–Aug); 10:30–5:30 Oct–Mar

🍴 Left Bank (€–€€)

Ⓜ Cité, St Michel

🚌 21, 24, 27, 38, 47, 85, 96

♿ Good

✋ Cathedral: free; treasure and towers: inexpensive

A classic view of Notre-Dame Cathedral, from pont de l'Archevêché

7
Orsay, Musée d'

Once a mainline railway station, the Musée d'Orsay has been successfully converted into one of Paris's three major art museums.

Built in 1900, the Gare d'Orsay was narrowly saved from demolition by a daring plan to turn it into a museum dedicated to all forms of art from 1848 to 1914, and intended as the chronological link between the Louvre and the Musée National d'Art Moderne. The Musée d'Orsay was inaugurated by President Mitterrand in 1986.

The main hall, with the station clock, was retained to create a sense of unity between painting, sculpture, architecture, design, photography and the cinema. The collections are spread over three levels:

• The Lower Level deals with the years from 1848 to 1880; small flights of steps lead off the central alleyway to various exhibition areas where major sculptures are displayed, including a group of graceful figures by Carpeaux entitled *La Danse*. On either side is a comprehensive collection of paintings of the same period – works by Ingres, Delacroix, Corot, Courbet and the Realists, as well as the beginning of Impressionism with early works by Monet, Manet, Pissarro etc.

• On the Upper Level is the prestigious Impressionist and post-Impressionist collection, undoubtedly the main attraction of the museum: masterpieces by Manet (*Olympia*), Degas (*Blue Dancers*), Sisley (*Snow in Louveciennes*), Renoir (*Bathers*), Monet (*The Houses of Parliament, Rouen Cathedral*), Cézanne (*The Card Players*), Van Gogh (*The Church at Auvers-sur-Oise*), Gauguin and the school of Pont-Aven, Matisse, Toulouse-Lautrec and many others.

• The Middle Level is dedicated to the period from 1870 to 1914 and includes important works by Rodin (*Balzac*), paintings by the Nabis school, as well as a comprehensive section on art nouveau (Lalique, Gallé, Guimard, Mackintosh and Wright).

The iron and glass former railway hall

www.musee-orsay.fr

✚ 28C3

✉ 62 rue de Lille (entrance rue de Légion d'Honneur), 75007 Paris

☎ 01 40 49 48 48 or 01 40 49 48 00

🕐 Tue–Sat 10–6, Sun 9–6; late night: Thu 9:45 (opens 9AM Jul–end-Sep). Closed Mon, 1 Jan, 1 May, 25 Dec

🍴 Restaurant (€), café (€)

Ⓜ Solférino

🚍 24, 63, 68, 69, 73, 83, 84, 94

♿ Very good

✋ Moderate, free first Sun each month

❓ Guided tours, shops, concerts, film shows

8
Les Quais

28C3

Quai du Louvre, quai de la Mégisserie (75001), quai de Gesvres, quai de l'Hôtel de Ville, quai des Célestins (75004), quai de la Tournelle, quai de Montebello, quai St-Michel (75005), quai des Grands Augustins, quai de Conti, quai Malaquais (75006), quai Voltaire, quai Anatole-France (75007)

Restaurants and cafés along the way, particularly near place du Châtelet and place de l'Hôtel de Ville on the Right Bank, and around place St-Michel on the Left Bank (€–€€€)

Pont-Neuf, Châtelet, Hôtel de Ville, Pont-Marie, St-Michel, Solférino

24 follows the Left Bank

Boat trips along the Seine from pont de l'Alma right round the islands

Street artists at work add to the timeless appeal of a stroll alongside the river

Walk along the banks of the Seine between the pont de la Concorde and the pont de Sully for some of Paris's finest views.

In 1992, the river banks from the pont d'Iéna, where the Tour Eiffel stands, to the pont de Sully, at the tip of the Ile Saint-Louis, were added to Unesco's list of World Heritage sites. Here the townscape has an indefinable charm inspired by the harmonious blend of colours: the pale greys and blues of the water and the sky, the soft green of the trees lining the embankment and the mellow stone colour of the historic buildings. Parisians have been strolling along the embankments for centuries, window-shopping, browsing through the *bouquinistes'* stalls or simply watching the activity on both sides of the river.

The Right Bank
Start from the pont du Carrousel and walk up-river past the imposing façade of the Louvre. From the pont Neuf, enjoy a fine view of the Conciergerie on the Ile de la Cité, or admire the birds and exotic fish on the quai de la Mégisserie. Continue past the Hôtel de Ville towards the lovely pont Marie leading to the peaceful Ile Saint-Louis. Cross over to the Left Bank.

The Left Bank
The familiar green boxes of the *bouquinistes* are here as well! Admire the stunning views of Notre-Dame and its magnificent flying buttresses. The quai Saint-Michel is a favourite haunt of students looking for second-hand books. Further on, stand on the pont des Arts for a romantic view of the historic heart of Paris before walking past the stately façade of the Musée d'Orsay towards the pont de la Concorde.

9
La Tour Eiffel

Paris's most famous landmark has been towering above the city for more than a hundred years, yet its universal appeal remains constant.

The Tour Eiffel was built by the engineer Gustave Eiffel as a temporary attraction for the 1889 World Exhibition. At the time, its 300-m height made it the tallest building in the world and an unprecedented technological achievement. It met with instant success, was celebrated by poets and artists, and its spindly silhouette was soon famous all over the world. In spite of this, it was nearly pulled down when the concession expired in 1909 but was saved because of its invaluable radio aerial, joined in 1957 by television aerials. It was later raised by another 20m to accommodate a meteorological station.

The iron frame weighs 7,000 tonnes, yet the pressure it exerts on the ground is only 4kg per square cm; 40 tonnes of paint are used to repaint it every seven years. To celebrate its one hundredth birthday, it was renovated and halogen lighting was installed making it even more spectacular at night than before.

There are three levels, all accessible by lift, or by stairs – first and second floors only. Information about the tower is available on the first floor (57m above ground); there are also a restaurant, a gift shop and a post office, where letters are post-marked 'Paris Tour Eiffel'.

The second floor (115m above ground) offers fine views of Paris, several boutiques and a restaurant appropriately named 'Jules Verne'.

For a spectacular aerial view of the capital go up to the third floor (276m above ground). There is also a reconstruction of Gustave Eiffel's study and panoramic viewing tables showing 360° photos of Paris with the city's landmarks.

There is a good view of the tower (with the statue of General Foch in the foreground) across the Seine from the place du Trocadéro

www.tour-eiffel.fr

28A3

Champ de Mars, 75007

01 44 11 23 23

Daily 9:30AM–11PM (stairs to 6:30) Sep–Jun; 9AM–midnight Jul–Aug

Restaurants (€–€€€)

Bir-Hakeim

42, 69, 72, 82, 87

Good

Lift: 1st–2nd floors inexpensive–moderate, 3rd floor expensive

10
La Villette

www.cite-sciences.fr
www.cite-musique.fr

✚ Off map 29F5

✉ Cité des Sciences et de l'Industrie, parc de la Villette, 30 avenue Corentin Cariou, 75019 Paris; Cité de la Musique, 221 avenue Jean Jaurès, 75019 Paris

☎ Cité des Sciences: 01 40 05 80 00; Cité de la Musique: information bookings 01 44 84 45 45

🕐 Cité des Sciences: Tue–Sat 10–6, Sun 10–7; closed 1 May, 25 Dec. Cité de la Musique: Tue–Sat 12–6, Sun 10–6

🍴 Restaurants near by (€–€€)

Ⓜ Cité des Sciences: Porte de la Villette; Cité de la Musique: Porte de Pantin

🚌 Cité des Sciences: 75, 139, 150, 152, PC; Cité de la Musique: 75, 151, PC

♿ Cité des Sciences: very good; Cité de la Musique, museum: excellent

✋ Cité des Sciences: expensive; Cité de la Musique: free, museum: moderate

❓ Cité des Sciences: exhibitions, lectures, shops; Cité de la Musique: themed tours, workshops, musical tours

La Géode, a huge hemispherical cinema

The Cité des Sciences et de l'Industrie and the Cité de la Musique revitalised the outer district of La Villette, turning it into a new cultural centre.

Situated just inside the boulevard périphérique, between the Porte de la Villette and the Porte de Pantin, the 30-ha parc de la Villette was laid out on the site of Paris's former abattoirs. This ultra-modern park includes two vast cultural complexes, one devoted to science and the other to music, themed gardens scattered with red metal follies and various children's activity areas. A long covered walk joins the main buildings.

Cité des Sciences et de l'Industrie

The abattoirs' former auction hall was transformed into a vast scientific complex surrounded by water in which the public is both spectator and actor. 'Explora' is a permanent exhibition centred on the earth and the universe, life, languages and communication, the use of natural resources and technological and industrial developments. The Cité des Enfants is a fascinating interactive world for children aged 3 to 12. There are also a planetarium, an aquarium, a 3-D cinema, a multimedia library, a research centre, a submarine, a simulation booth (Cinaxe), in which spectators are able to live through the action of a film, and La Géode, a huge sphere equipped with a hemispherical screen that shows films on scientific subjects.

Cité de la Musique

The focal point of the Cité de la Musique is the vast square in front of the Grande Halle where concerts and exhibitions are held. On the left of the square is the new music and dance conservatory, while the triangular building on the right houses concerts halls and a museum (see Musée de la Musique ➤ 63).

What
To See

Above: *Institut de France clock detail*

PARIS

Porte de Champerret
AVENUE DE LA PORTE DE CHAMPERRET
BLVD BERTHIER
Station
Pont Cardinet
Square des
Batignolles
Cimetière de
Montmartre
AVENUE DE VILLIERS
17
BOULEVARD DES BATIGNOLLES
AVENUE DE WAGRAM
BOULEVARD DE COURCELLES
Musée
Cernuschi
Gare
St-Lazare
5
BOULEVARD GOUVION ST-CYR
PORTE DES TERNES
Parc de
Monceau
Musée
Nissim
de Camondo
St-Augustin
RUE DE LA PÉPINIÈRE
Palais des
Congrès
RUE DU FAUBOURG ST-HONORÉ
Musée
Jacquemart
André
BLVD HAUSSMANN
Musée
Fragonard
Grande Arche
de la Défense
AVE DE LA GRANDE ARMÉE
AVE DE
FRIEDLAND
BLVD HAUSSMANN
Opéra
Garnier
PORTE
MAILLOT
Arc de Triomphe
Lido
PLACE CHARLES
DE GAULLE
ÉTOILE
8
PLACE
DE LA
MADELEINE
AVENUE FOCH
Office
du
Tourisme
AVENUE DES CHAMPS ELYSÉES
Palais de l'Élysée
Église de la
Madeleine
BLVD DE LA
MADELEINE
4
AVENUE VICTOR HUGO
CHAMPS ELYSÉES
PLACE
VENDÔME
St-Roch
Musée
National des Arts
Asiatiques-Guimet
Palais
Galliera
Grand
Palais
Palais de la
Découverte
Petit
Palais
Jeu de
Paume
RUE DE RIVOLI
16
Musée Marmottan
Palais de Tokyo
Musée d'Art Moderne
ALBERT I ER
COURS LA REINE
PLACE
DE LA
CONCORDE
Orangerie
Jardin des
Tuileries
Palais de
Chaillot
PONT DE L'ALMA
Seine
PONT DES INVALIDES
QUAI DES TUILERIES
Jardins du
Trocadéro
QUAI BRANLY
QUAI D'ORSAY
QUAI D'ORSAY
QUAI ANATOLE FRANCE
Musée du
Louvre
Maison de
Balzac
Tour Eiffel
3
Esplanade
des
Invalides
Assemblée
Nationale-
Palais
Bourbon
Musée
d'Orsay
QUAI VOLTAIRE
École des
Beaux Arts
Parc du
7
Hôtel des
Invalides
Musée
Rodin
Musée
Maillol
BOULEVARD
Champ
de Mars
AVE DE TOURVILLE
RUE DE VARENNE
St-Germain
des Prés
École
Militaire
6
UNESCO
AVE DE BRETEUIL
RUE DE SÈVRES
AVENUE ÉMILE ZOLA
BLVD GARIBALDI
Jardin du
Luxembourg
2
BLVD PASTEUR
RUE DE VAUGIRARD
BLVD
RASPAIL
RUE LECOURBE
15
RUE DE VAUGIRARD
BLVD DU MONTPARNASSE
RUE D'AUGIRARD
BLVD DE
VAUGIRARD
Tour
Montparnasse
MONTPARNASSE
RUE
LEBLANC
Gare
Montparnasse
Cimetière
du
Montparnasse
BOULEVARD VICTOR
RUE DE LA PLAINE
14
RUE FROIDEVAUX
PORTE DE
SÈVRES
Parc des
1
BOULEVARD LEFEBVRE
Expositions
BOULEVARD PÉRIPHÉRIQUE
PORTE DE
LA PLAINE

A   B   C

PARIS

MONTMARTRE

- Musée de Montmartre
- Basilique du Sacré-Cœur
- Bal du Moulin Rouge
- **9**
- **18**
- Gare du Nord
- La Villette, Musée de la Musique
- **19**
- Parc des Buttes Chaumont
- Musée Baccarat
- Gare de l'Est
- Folies Bergère
- Musée Grévin
- **10**
- Hôpital St-Louis
- Palais de la Bourse
- **2**
- Bibliothèque Nationale
- Conservatoire des Arts et Métiers
- **20**
- Hôtel des Postes
- St-Eustache
- Palais Royal
- **1**
- **3**
- Comédie Française
- Bourse de Commerce
- Les Halles
- Centre Georges Pompidou-Centre National d'Art et de Culture
- Cimetière du Père Lachaise
- **11**
- Palais du Louvre
- Forum
- Tour St-Jacques
- Musée de la Chasse et de la Nature
- Archives Nationales
- Théâtre Musical
- Théâtre de la Ville
- Musée d'Histoire de France
- Musée Picasso
- Musée Cognacq-Jay
- Institut de France
- Conciergerie Palais de Justice Ste-Chapelle
- Musée Carnavalet
- MARAIS
- Musée Delacroix
- Préf. de Police
- Île de la Cité
- Hôtel de Ville
- **4**
- Église St-Paul-St-Louis
- Maison de Victor Hugo
- St-Sulpice
- Hôtel Dieu
- Cathédrale Notre-Dame
- Île St-Louis
- Opéra Bastille
- Palais du Luxembourg
- Musée Nat du Moyen-Age
- **12**
- QUARTIER LATIN
- Sorbonne
- Viaduc des Arts
- Panthéon
- St Étienne-du-Mont
- Institut du Monde Arabe
- Gare de Lyon
- **5**
- Mosquée
- Jardin des Plantes
- Observatoire
- Muséum National d'Histoire Naturelle
- Gare d'Austerlitz
- Palais Omnisports de Bercy
- Manufacture des Gobelins
- **13**

29

Paris

The city of Paris has always played its role of capital of France to the full. It is the place where the French nation's future is decided, where revolutions began in the past and where major political, economic and social changes are traditionally launched. This is as true today as it ever was, in spite of many attempts at decentralisation.

Parisian life reflects the city's leading role in many different ways: the numerous trade exhibitions and international conferences taking place every year testify to its economic and potitical dynamism and healthy competitive spirit. Paris is continually on the move in all fields of human activity: its architectural heritage is constantly expanding and it is proudly setting new trends in the arts, in gastronomy and in fashion. Paris is also a cosmopolitan metropolis where many ethnic groups find the necessary scope to express their differences.

> *'If you are lucky enough to have lived in Paris as a young man, then wherever you go for the rest of your life, it stays with you, for Paris is a movable feast.'*

ERNEST HEMINGWAY
A Movable Feast (1964)

ARRONDISSEMENTS

Paris is divided into 20 arrondissements

Exploring Paris

It is tempting for visitors to allow themselves to be whisked off from one major sight to the next without ever getting the feel of the true Paris. You must wander off the beaten track to discover the city's hidden assets, which are often tucked away around unexpected corners.

La Marseillaise frieze on the Arc De Triomphe

To get the best out of Paris, you should travel by métro or bus from one main area to the next and then explore the neighbourhood on foot.

Each district has its own character-istics: Montmartre and Montparnasse are associated with artists while the Marais is inhabited by a trendy middle class; the splendid mansions of the Faubourg St-Germain have been taken over by government ministries but St-Germain-des-Prés and the Quartier Latin are still the favourite haunt of intellectuals and students. There are also several colourful ethnic areas: Chinatown in the 13th *arrondissement*, the African district north of the Gare du Nord and the Jewish quarter in the Marais.

Some areas are best avoided at night: around the Gare du Nord, Les Halles and the Grands Boulevards between République and Richelieu-Drouot.

What to See in Paris

PONT ALEXANDRE III ✪

This is Paris's most ornate bridge, inaugurated for the 1900 World Exhibition and named after the Tsar of Russia to celebrate the Franco-Russian alliance. Its sole arch (107m) spanning the Seine is in line with the Invalides on the Left Bank while, on the Right Bank, the avenue Winston Churchill leads straight to the Champs-Elysées, passing the Grand and Petit Palais. The bridge is decorated with exuberant allegorical sculptures surmounted by gilt horses.

ARC DE TRIOMPHE ✪✪✪

This stately monument stands in the middle of the circular place Charles de Gaulle, formerly known as the place de l'Etoile because of the 12 avenues that radiate from it. Commissioned by Napoleon, it was completed by France's last reigning monarch and finally dedicated to the memory of an unknown soldier of the Republic who died during World War I.

Looking at the harmonious proportions of its familiar silhouette and its splendid carvings you forget its megalomaniac origins. It stands in line with two other arches – the Arc de Triomphe du Carrousel near the Louvre and the Grande Arche de la Défense. At 50m high, the Arc de Triomphe is twice the height of the former and only half that of the latter.

From the top there is a 360 degree panorama, with, in the foreground, the 12 avenues reaching out like tentacles towards the city beyond.

ARMÉE, MUSÉE DE L' (➤ 19)

🚹 28B3
✉ Cours La Reine/Quai d'Orsay
🚇 Invalides, Champs-Elysées-Clémenceau
🚌 63, 83

🚹 28A4
✉ Place Charles de Gaulle, 75008 Paris
☎ 01 55 37 73 77
🕐 Oct–Mar: 10AM–10:30PM; Apr–Sep: 10AM–11PM, closed 1 Jan, 1 May, 25 Dec
🍴 Choice of restaurants near by (€–€€€)
🚇 Charles de Gaulle-Etoile
🚌 73
♿ Very good
✋ Moderate
❓ Video, shops

A ceremony takes place at the Arc de Triomphe every Armistice Day

ART MODERNE DE LA VILLE DE PARIS, MUSÉE D' ⭐⭐

The Palais de Tokyo housing the modern art collections was built for the 1937 World Exhibition; significantly, one of the main exhibits is a huge work called *La Fée Electricité*, painted by Raoul Dufy for the 'Light pavilion' at the Exhibition. Most of the major artisistic trends of the 20th century are represented; During the restructuring of the museum, part of its collections are exhibited in other museums and local town halls throughout the capital; phone for details or consult the museum's website.

www.mam.paris.fr
✚ 28A4
✉ 11 avenue du Président Wilson, 75116 Paris
☎ 01 53 67 40 00
🕐 Closed for restructuring, reopening 2005
🍴 Cafe (€)
🚇 Iéna, Alma-Marceau
🚌 32, 42, 63, 72, 80, 92
♿ Very good
💰 Inexpensive
❓ Guided tours (reservations necessary)

Exciting exhibits at the Musée d'Art Moderne

ARTS ASIATIQUES-GUIMET, MUSÉE NATIONAL DES/PANTHÉON BOUDDHIQUE ⭐⭐

The renovated and extended Musée Guimet is now one of the most outstanding museums of Asian art in the world. Its collections, spanning 5,000 years, illustrate all the major civilisations of the Asian continent, with special emphasis on calligraphy, painting, gold plate and textiles. In addition, carefully restored monumental works from Cambodia and Afghanistan are on display for the first time.

www.museeguimet.fr
✚ 28A4
✉ Museum: 6 place d'Iéna; Panthéon Bouddhique: 19 avenue d'Iéna, 75116
☎ 01 56 52 53 00
🕐 Wed–Mon 10–6
🚇 Boissière, Iéna
🚌 22, 30, 32, 63, 82
♿ Excellent 💰 Moderate

ARTS DÉCORATIFS, MUSÉE DES ⭐⭐

Founded in the 19th century in order to display 'Beauty in function', the Museum of decorative arts, housed in the Marsan wing of the Louvre, is gradually reopening its departments after undergoing major restructuring. The Medieval and Renaissance collections include remarkable altarpieces, religious paintings, 16th-century stained glass objects of daily life, as well as fine tapestries exhibited in rotaiton. The reopening of the remaining 17th-, 18th-, 19th- and 20th-century collections is scheduled for 2005.

www.ucad.fr
✚ 28C3
✉ 107 rue de Rivoli; 75001
☎ 01 44 55 57 50
🕐 Tue–Fri 11–6, Sat–Sun 10–6
🍴 The main Louvre near by
♿ Good 🚇 Palais-Royal
🚌 21, 27, 39, 48, 67, 69, 72, 81
💰 Inexpensive

ARTS ET MÉTIERS-TECHNIQUES, MUSÉE DES NATIONAL ⭐⭐

Entirely renovated, this museum is devoted to the artistic aspect of scientific and technical achievements.

✚ 29E4 ✉ 60 rue Réaumur, 75003 Paris ☎ 01 53 01 82 00
🕐 Tue–Sun 10–6 (Thu to 9.30pm) 💰 Moderate **33**

One of the historical figures decorating the Palais-Bourbon, seat of the Assemblée Nationale

ASSEMBLÉE NATIONALE PALAIS-BOURBON ✪

The façade of this neo-classical building, housing the lower house of the French parliament, echoes that of the Madeleine across the place de la Concorde. Completed by Louis XV's famous architect Gabriel, the Palais-Bourbon still bears the name of the French royal family to whom it once belonged. Guided tours (identity document required) include the chamber, where members of parliament sit on benches arranged in semicircular tiers, several reception rooms and the library, richly decorated by Delacroix.

BACCARAT, MUSÉE ✪

The prestigious collections of Baccarat crystal are housed in one of the last 19th-century post-houses in Paris. More than one thousand pieces illustrate the evolution of styles and manufacturing techniques since 1764: vases, chandeliers, perfume bottles and various other objects including candelabra ordered by Tsar Nicholas II of Russia. The most fascinating exhibits are probably the unique pieces specially created by Baccarat for various World Exhibitions since 1855.

BALZAC, MAISON DE ✪

This is the house in which Honoré de Balzac lived from 1840 to 1847, while he was writing the series of novels *La Comédie Humaine*. The house contains numerous mementos of his life and work, such as manuscripts, letters, original drawings and prints and a plaster cast that Rodin used as a study for the monumental statue now standing in Montparnasse. Balzac used the backdoor in the picturesque rue Berton when he needed to avoid the bailiffs!

BASTILLE ✪✪

The place de la Bastille is forever associated with the French Revolution, since it was here that it all began. The dreaded fortress was stormed by the people of Paris on 14 July 1789 and later razed to the ground; its outline can be seen on the paving stones covering the entire square. In the centre stands a 50m-high column erected in memory of the victims of the 1830 and 1848 Revolutions, who were buried beneath the base and whose names are carved on the shaft. The column is surmounted by the gilt winged figure of the *Spirit of Liberty* by Dumont.

The new Paris opera house, one of President Mitterrand's 'Grands projets', was inaugurated for the bicentenary of the 1789 Revolution. It was the subject of bitter controversy from the start as running costs proved too high for an establishment intended as a popular opera house. Designed by the Canadian architect Carlos Ott, the **Opéra National de Paris-Bastille** is a harmonious building with a curved façade in several shades of grey that glitters in the sun and gently glows at night. The acoustics of the main auditorium, which can accommodate 2,700 spectators, are superb and the stage is one of the most sophisticated in the world.

Just south of the opera house, a disused railway viaduct has been converted into a series of workshops and showrooms illustrating a number of traditional crafts known as the **Viaduc des Arts**; the Ateliers du Cuivre et de l'Argent (copper and silver workshops) are particularly interesting and there is a small museum.

✚ 29F2

Opéra National de Paris-Bastille
- ✉ Place de la Bastille, 75012 Paris
- ☎ Recorded information: 01 40 01 19 70
- ⏱ Listen to the recorded information; closed Sun
- 🍴 Bar
- Ⓜ Bastille
- 🚌 20, 29, 65, 69, 76, 86, 87, 91
- ♿ Good 🅿 Moderate
- ❓ Guided tours, shops

Viaduc des Arts
- ✉ 9–129 avenue Daumesnil, 75012 Paris
- ⏱ Variable; most workshops open Sun
- 🍴 Near by (€)
- Ⓜ Bastille, Ledru-Rollin, Reuilly-Diderot

Above: *the Bastille monument*

Left: *the Governor of the Bastille being led to the town hall by the revolutionaries*

35

Food & Drink

In France, eating is an art that reaches its highest expression in Paris, for here the diversity and know-how of traditional regional cuisine are combined with a creative spirit stimulated by a strong cosmopolitan influence. In recent years, a growing awareness of the need for healthier living has prompted the invention of *nouvelle cuisine* and contributed to change the Parisians' eating habits.

Musée du Vin

✉ 5 square Charles Dickens, 75016 Paris

☎ 01 45 25 63 26

🕐 Tue–Sun 10–6

🍴 Nice bistro (€)

🚇 Passy

♿ Good

💶 Moderate; free for visitors eating in the restaurant

↔ Maison de Balzac (► 34)

❓ Guided tours, bookshop, gift shop

Opposite: *watching the world go by from pavement cafés is a national pastime; traditional baguettes, bought daily; tarte au citron, a popular dessert; expresso coffee – small, dark and strong*

Below: *fresh fish in Le Marais*

Eating Parisian Style

The traditional French breakfast of bread, butter and jam with a large cup of *café au lait* (white coffee) has to a large extent given way to cereals and milk with black coffee, tea or chocolate. The traditional fresh croissants are often a weekend treat, when people breakfast *en famille*.

The majority of working people have lunch out. Cafés and bistros overflow onto the pavements in spring and summer and overworked waiters are continually calling out *un steak frites* (steak and chips) at the tops of their voices, as Parisians order their favourite lunchtime dish. Some of the trendiest places to have lunch are *bars à huîtres* (oyster bars, serving a variety of seafood) and cyber cafés where you can have a snack and a drink while surfing the Internet!

Dinner at home around 8PM is the first relaxing meal of the day, enjoyed with family or friends; it starts with hors-d'oeuvre, finishes with cheese or a sweet and may include a freshly prepared dish bought from a local *traiteur* (delicatessen), accompanied by a glass of wine.

Shopping for Food

Parisians are still very fond of their local street markets where they can buy fresh vegetables and fruit as well as cheese, charcuterie, fish and meat. One traditional item which is still going strong is the *baguette*, the light and crisp bread that is better in Paris than anywhere else in France!

Eating Out

Eating out is one of the Parisians' favourite forms of entertainment as conviviality is as important as the food itself. Friday night and Saturday night are the most popular evenings, while families with children tend to go out for Sunday lunch. Parisian cuisine includes a wide choice of regional and traditional dishes, although the tendency nowadays is to lighten sauces. Typical Parisian dishes are *soupe à l'oignon gratinée* (onion soup *au gratin*) and *pieds de cochon* (grilled pig's trotters), traditionally eaten near Les Halles when this was the chief food market in Paris. Oysters and seafood in general are also very popular, judging by the numerous take-away seafood stalls outside restaurants in the city centre.

Wine is a must with any good meal, preceded by an aperitif, which may consist of port, whisky or champagne. A *digestif* (brandy, Cointreau or any other liqueur) is served with coffee at the end of the meal.

Musée du Vin

Anyone interested in wine should visit this museum, appropriately housed in the old cellars of Passy Abbey. It illustrates the history of wine in France and the main wine-producing areas, and has a collection of tools, bottles, and wax figures. An added inducement is the opportunity for some wine-tasting.

The Galerie Vivienne, a charming arcade linked to the Bibliothèque Nationale de France

www.bnf.fr
➕ 29D4
✉ Richelieu: 58 rue de Richelieu, 75002 Paris; François Mitterrand: quai François Mauriac, 75013 Paris
☎ Richelieu: 01 53 79 59 59 rguided tours: 01 53 79 86 87; François Mitterrand: 01 53 79 59 59
🕐 Richelieu: Galeries and Crypt: Tue–Sat 10–7, Sun 12–7. Cabinet des Médailles: daily 1–5; Sun 12–6. François Mitterrand: visits of the building on Tue–Sat 2, Sun 3 by appointment only.
🍴 Richelieu: restaurant in Galerie Vivienne (€)
🚇 Richelieu: Bourse, Palais-Royal–Musée du Louvre; François Mitterrand: Quai de la Gare
🚌 Richelieu: 29, 39, 48; François Mitterrand: 62, 89
♿ Very good
💶 Richelieu: moderate; François Mitterrand: free

BIBLIOTHÈQUE NATIONALE DE FRANCE ⭐

The national library is seen by the French as a symbol of their culture. Until 1996, the BN, as Parisians call it, was housed in Cardinal Mazarin's former palace situated at the back of the Palais-Royal, extended many times and now stretching from the rue de Richelieu to the rue Vivienne. However, with around 13 million books and as many prints and photographs, it had long been overcrowded. The building of a new library along the river in the 13th arrondissement was President Mitterrand's last 'Grand Projet'. The BNF, as it is now called, occupies two sites known as 'Richelieu' and 'François Mitterrand'.

The new library houses the huge stock of printed books and documents and is intended to serve as a public library and a research centre equipped with the most modern means of data transmission. Four corner towers looking like open books surround an imposing base with a central garden where the reading rooms are situated.

The Richelieu building houses manuscripts, prints and medals and holds exhibitions in the Galerie Mansart (Galerie de Photographie), the Galerie Mazarine (which has a magnificent painted ceiling) and the Crypte. The Cabinet des Médailles et des Antiques displays coins and medals from antiquity to the present day as well as *objets d'art*, cameos and bronzes from the former royal collections.

Two charming arcades linked to the library, the Galerie Vivienne and the Galerie Colbert, offer an unexpected insight into Parisian social life in the 19th century.

CARNAVALET, MUSÉE ✪✪

This museum retraces the history of Paris from antiquity to the present day, and is worth visiting for the building alone: a beautiful Renaissance mansion, one of the oldest in Le Marais, remodelled in the 17th century. The Hôtel Carnavalet was the residence of diarist, Madame de Sévigné, who depicted Parisian society at the time of Louis XIV with a great deal of humour. Note the 16th-century lions guarding the entrance and Louis XIV's statue by Coysevox in the centre of the courtyard. In 1989, the museum was linked to the nearby Hôtel Le Peletier de St Fargeau, which dates from the late 17th century. The Hôtel Carnavalet deals with the period from the origins of the city to 1789, with mementoes of Madame de Sévigné and splendid Louis XV and Louis XVI furniture. The Hôtel Le Peletier de St Fargeau houses collections from 1789 to the present day. The Revolution is extensively illustrated, while the 19th and 20th centuries are represented by a number of reconstructions such as Marcel Proust's bedroom and the art nouveau reception room of the Café de Paris.

✚ 29E3
✉ 23 rue de Sévigné, 75003 Paris
☎ 01 44 59 58 58
🕐 Tue–Sun 10–6; closed some public hols
🍴 Restaurants and cafés near by in rue des Francs-Bourgeois (€–€€€)
Ⓜ Saint-Paul
🚌 29, 96
♿ Some weehlchair access; tel: 01 44 59 58 31
🎟 Free, except for some temporary exhibitions
❓ Guided tours, shops

The courtyard of the Musée Carnavalet

CENTRE GEORGES POMPIDOU (▶ 16, TOP TEN)

CERNUSCHI, MUSÉE ✪

The banker and art collector Henri Cernuschi bequeathed his elegant private mansion to the city of Paris at the end of the 19th century. Situated on the edge of the parc Monceau, the building houses Cernuschi's superb collection of ancient Chinese art on the ground floor (terracottas, bronzes, jades and ceramics) and contemporary traditional Chinese paintings on the first floor.

✚ 28B5
✉ 7 avenue Velasquez, 75008 Paris
☎ 01 45 63 50 75
🕐 Closed for restructuring until 2005
Ⓜ Villiers 🚌 30, 94
♿ Good 🎟 Inexpensive

Magnificent bronzes, pools and fountains front the Palais de Chaillot

www.mnhn.fr
www.musee-marine.fr
➕ 28A3
✉ Place du Trocadéro, 75116 Paris
☎ Musée de l'Homme: 01 44 05 72 72; Musée de la Marine: 01 53 65 69 69
🕐 Musée de l'Homme: Mon, Wed–Fri 9:45–5:15,Sat–Sun 10–6:30; closed bank hols. Musée de la Marine: Wed–Mon 10–6; closed 1 Jan, 1 May, 25 Dec
🚇 Trocadéro
🚌 22, 30, 32, 63, 72, 82
♿ Musée de l'Homme: none; Musée de la Marine: good
🍴 Both museums: moderate
❓ Both museums have a bookshop; guided tours in Musée de la Marine

CHAILLOT, PALAIS DE ⭐⭐

This imposing architectural complex on top of a hill overlooking the river and facing the Tour Eiffel across the pont d'Iéna offers magnificent views and houses two interesting museums.

Designed for the 1937 World Exhibition, the building consists of two separate pavilions with curved wings, on either side of a vast terrace decorated with monumental statues. Just below, the tiered Jardins du Trocadéro extend to the edge of the river. The ornamental fountain is particularly impressive at night when the powerful spray of water shines under the spotlights.

The Musée de l'Homme, devoted to Man as a species, is being restructured over five years. Meanwhile, three exhibitions give a foretaste of what the new museum will be like: La Nuit des Temps (the human adventure), Six milliards d'hommes (the growth of the world's population) and Tous parents, tous différents (the similarities and diversity of mankind).

The Musée de la Marine is devoted to French maritime history from the 18th century onwards. The extensive collections show the development of navigational skills and include beautiful models of 18th-century sailing ships; they also provide an insight into the modern navy and retrace the history of maritime transport and great expeditions across the world.

The east wing was seriously damaged by fire in 1997 and the two museums it contained are now closed. The Musée des Monuments Français will reopen once building work has finished, whereas the Musée du Cinéma Henri Langlois will probably move to new premises in the former American Center in Bercy.

CHAMPS-ELYSÉES, LES (➤ 17, TOP TEN)

CHASE ET DE LA NATURE, MUSÉE DE LA (➤ 56)

CITÉ, ILE DE LA ✪✪✪

The Ile de la Cité is not only the historic centre of Paris, it is also a place of exceptional natural beauty and an architectural gem.

The Celtic tribe the Parisii settled on the largest island in an area known as Lutetia, which under the Romans expanded onto the Left Bank of the Seine. Nevertheless, the island (the Cité), which the king of the Franks chose as his capital in 508, remained for 1,000 years the seat of royal, judicial and religious power. During the Middle Ages, the Ile de la Cité was an important intellectual centre as its cathedral schools attracted students from all over Europe. Even after the kings of France left the royal palace for larger premises on the right bank, the Cité lost none of its symbolic importance and remains to this day the 'guardian' of 2,000 years of history.

The appearance of the Cité has, of course, changed considerably over the years; in the 19th century, the centre of the island was cleared and the vast square in front of Notre-Dame Cathedral created. At the other end of the island, the Conciergerie (►44) and Sainte-Chapelle (►73) are the only remaining parts of the medieval royal palace, now incorporated in the huge Palais de Justice.

29E2

Ile de la Cité, 75001 and 75004 Paris

Restaurants and cafés (€–€€) on the island and on the Right and Left banks

Cité, Pont Neuf, St-Michel, Châtelet, Hôtel de Ville

21, 24, 27, 38, 47, 58, 70, 85, 96

A view of Ile de la Cité and pont Neuf

41

A Walk Along the Seine & On the Islands

This relatively compact area offers stately historic buildings, breathtaking views, provincial charm and the liveliness of a great city.

Start from the place du Châtelet on the Right Bank.

The monumental fountain was commissioned by Napoleon on his return from Egypt.

Walk along the quai de Gesvres, then across the pont Notre-Dame.

The flower market on the place Louis Lépine is a refreshing sight. On Sunday, flowers are replaced by birds.

Walk east along the embankment, turn right into rue des Ursins then left and left again.

The narrow streets of the medieval cathedral precinct have some old houses. At the tip of the island is an underground memorial to the victims of Nazi concentration camps.

Cross over to the Ile Saint-Louis and turn left, following the quai de Bourbon.

Enjoy the peaceful atmosphere of this sought-after residential area (➤ 72).

Turn right into rue des Deux Ponts and cross over to the Left Bank. Walk west to the square Viviani then cross rue St-Jacques into rue St-Séverin.

This is one of the oldest parts of the Quartier Latin. The Gothic Church of St-Séverin has a magnificent interior.

From the place St-Michel, cross back on to the Ile de la Cité.

Sainte-Chapelle (➤ 73) is very close. The place Dauphine at the western end of the island is another haven of peace. Admire the view from the pont Neuf, Paris's oldest bridge.

Cross over to the Right Bank and the pont Neuf métro station.

Distance
4km

Time
2–4 hours depending on church visits

Start point
Place du Châtelet
✚ 29D3
🚇 Châtelet or 🚌 21, 38, 85, 96

End point
Pont Neuf
✚ 29D3
🚇 Pont Neuf or 🚌 21, 58, 67, 70

Lunch
Le Vieux Bistrot
✉ 14 rue du Cloître-Notre-Dame, 75004 Paris
☎ 01 43 54 18 95

Left: *Pont Neuf*
Below: *Place du Châtelet salutes Napoleon's Egyptian campaign*

Macabre associations always attract crowds, and La Conciergerie, Paris's oldest prison, is no exception

+ 29E3
⊠ Hôtel Donon, 8 rue
  Elzévir, 75003 Paris
☎ 01 40 27 07 21
⏰ 10–6; closed Mon and
  public hols
🍴 Near by (€–€€)
Ⓜ Saint-Paul 🚌 29, 96
♿ None 🎫 Free
❓ Guided tours, bookshop

COGNACQ-JAY, MUSÉE ⭐⭐

The collections of 18th-century European art bequeathed to the city of Paris by Ernest Cognacq and his wife Louise Jay, founders of the Samaritaine department stores, are displayed in one of the beautiful mansions of Le Marais. The refinement of the Enlightenment period is illustrated by the works of French artists Watteau, Chardin, Fragonard and La Tour, and also by Tiepolo, Guardi and Reynolds. The Rembrandt adds a welcome contrasting note. Various *objets d'art*, including Saxe and Sèvres porcelain, are exhibited in glass cabinets.

+ 28D3
⊠ 2 boulevard du Palais,
  75001 Paris
☎ 01 53 40 60 97
⏰ Daily 9:30–6; closed 1
  Jan, 1 May, 25 Dec
Ⓜ Cité, Châtelet
🚌 21, 24, 27, 38, 58, 85, 81,
  85, 96, Balabus
♿ None
🎫 Moderate
❓ Guided tours, bookshop

LA CONCIERGERIE ⭐⭐

For most people, the name 'Conciergerie' suggests crowds of innocent prisoners waiting to be taken to the guillotine. Nowadays, its familiar round towers covered with conical slate roofs and the square clock tower, which housed the first public clock in Paris, are one of the most picturesque sights of the Ile de la Cité. The Conciergerie is the last remaining authentic part of a 14th-century royal complex, administered by a 'concierge' or governor. The twin towers marked the main entrance to the palace. In the late 14th century, the Conciergerie was turned into a prison but it only acquired a sinister connotation during the Revolution, when it held a number of famous prisoners, including Queen Marie-Antoinette, Madame du Barry and the poet André Chénier, as well as Danton and Robespierre.

The visit includes the original guards' room, a magnificent great hall with Gothic vaulting and kitchens with monumental fireplaces. There is also a reconstruction of Marie-Antoinette's cell.

CONCORDE, PLACE DE LA ✪✪✪

This is undoubtedly the most impressive square in Paris: its stately elegance, its size and its magnificent views are simply breathtaking. Built in the mid-18th century to celebrate Louis XV 'the beloved', it was designed by Gabriel who erected two classical pavilions on either side of the rue Royale; its octagonal shape is emphasised by eight allegorical statues representing major French cities.

The pink granite obelisk from Luxor, offered to the French nation by the viceroy of Egypt in 1836, is at the centre of the square, flanked by two graceful fountains. Two magnificent vistas open up: one towards the Champs-Elysées and Le Louvre beyond the beautiful gates of the Jardin des Tuileries, the other towards the Madeleine at the end of the rue Royale and the Assemblée Nationale across the pont de la Concorde.

✚ 28C4
✉ 75008 Paris
Ⓜ Concorde
🚌 42, 73, 84, 94

Decorative architecture and statuary (left and above) grace place de la Concorde

EUGÈNE DELACROIX, MUSÉE NATIONAL ✪

The old-world charm of the tiny rue de Furstenberg, hidden behind the Church of St-Germain-des-Prés, is the perfect setting for a museum devoted to one of the major French Romantic painters. Delacroix lived and worked here until the end of his life and, besides a few paintings, the place is full of mementoes of the artist, letters, sketches...and his palette. There is also a bookshop. It is well worth taking time to explore the picturesque neighbourhood and the open market in rue de Buci.

www.musee-delacroix.fr
✚ 29D3
✉ 6 rue de Furstenberg, 75006 Paris
☎ 01 44 41 86 50
🕐 9:30–5; closed Tue and public holidays
Ⓜ St-Germain-des-Prés
🚌 39, 48, 63, 95
♿ None 💶 Inexpensive

45

28C3

75007 Paris

For the museums'
opening times, see the
relevant entries

Cafés and restaurants
near by in boulevard St-
Germain (€–€€)

Varenne, Rue du Bac

69, 83, 84, 94

FAUBOURG ST-GERMAIN

This 'suburb' is today one of the most elegant districts of central Paris.

Its name came from the nearby Abbaye de St-Germain-des-Prés to which it belonged in medieval times. University students loved to stroll through fields and meadows stretching down to the river west of the abbey and the area remained in its natural state until the 18th century, when it became fashionable for the aristocracy and the wealthy middle class to have mansions built there by the famous architects of the time. Today, a few streets have retained some of their past elegance even though most of the mansions have now been taken over by ministries and foreign embassies.

The rue de Varenne (a distortion of *garenne*, the French word for warren, which confirms the area's rural origins!), is lined with the famous Hôtel Matignon, built in 1721 and now the Prime Minister's residence, and the Hôtel Biron, better known as the Musée Rodin (➤ 70). The parallel rue de Grenelle is equally interesting for its wealth of authentic architecture, including the Hôtel de Villars, which is now the town hall of the 7th *arrondissement*. Further along the street, on the opposite side, there is an interesting museum (No 59) devoted to the sculptor Maillol (➤ 55) and, next to it, the beautiful Fontaine des Quatre Saisons (Fountain of the Four Seasons).

Typical Parisian apartments, four to six storeys high, in Faubourg-St-Germain. Uniformly painted in shades of white and grey, the mansions date from the 17th and 18th centuries

Did you know ?

Queen Marie-Antoinette's dressmaker is said to be at the origin of what we now call haute couture, *but the first real fashion houses date from the second half of the 19th century. Their progress was so rapid that an entire pavilion was devoted to high fashion at the 1900 World Exhibition!*

Faubourg St-Honoré is not for those on a budget

FAUBOURG ST-HONORÉ

This other 'suburb', this time on the Right Bank, is centred on the very long street of the same name, running parallel to the Champs-Elysées and famous for its *haute couture* establishments and luxury boutiques as well as for the Palais de l'Elysée, the official residence of the French president.

Leading fashion houses have been established in the area for over a hundred years: Louis Féraud, Christian Lacroix and Lanvin are still in the rue du Faubourg St-Honoré, but the majority are now in the avenue Montaigne across the Champs-Elysées. Opposite the British Embassy, No 54 opens into a couple of courtyards surrounded by boutiques selling beautiful furniture, *objets d'art*, paintings etc. Many modern art galleries line the perpendicular avenue Matignon, while the avenue Gabriel, which runs along the Champs-Elysées gardens past the American Embassy, makes a peaceful stroll through this select area.

- 28B4
- 75008 Paris
- St-Philippe-du-Roule, Madeleine
- 52
- A stamp market takes place near the Rond-Point des Champs-Elysées on Thu, Sat and Sun 9–7

GALLIÉRA, MUSÉE

This museum of fashion is appropriately housed in a neo-Renaissance mansion dating from the late 19th century, the Palais Galliéra. Its rich collections of urban fashion, are shown in temporary exhibitions from the 18th century to the present and are continually being extended with donations from prestigious fashion houses (Dior, Yves St-Laurent) and well-known personalities. In addition to the costumes (several thousands in all), there are etchings and photographs connected with fashion.

- Off map 28A4
- Palais Galliéra, 10 avenue Pierre Ier de Serbie, 75016 Paris
- 01 56 52 86 00
- 10–6; closed Mon
- Iéna 32, 63, 72, 92
- None   Moderate
- Children's workshops

47

+ 29E1
✉ 42 avenue des Gobelins, 75013 Paris
☎ 01 44 54 19 33/ 01 44 08 52 00
🕐 Tue, Wed, Thu guided tours only at 2 and 2:45; closed public hols
Ⓜ Les Gobelins
🚌 27, 47, 83, 91
♿ None
👋 Moderate

GOBELINS, MANUFACTURE NATIONALE DES ✪

The former royal tapestry factory, founded by Colbert in 1664 to make beautiful tapestries for the royal household, is still going strong. Priceless works of art, based on paintings by artists such as Le Brun and Boucher and, more recently, Lurçat and Picasso, have been produced in the workshops over the last three centuries. Techniques have hardly changed since the 17th century and looms are either upright (*haute lice* method) or horizontal (*basse lice* method). The 17th-century buildings also house the Savonnerie carpet factory, founded in 1604, and the Beauvais tapestry factory, founded at the same time as the Gobelins.

LA GRANDE ARCHE DE LA DÉFENSE (➤ 18, TOP TEN)

GRAND PALAIS ✪✪

+ 28B4
✉ Galeries Nationales: avenue du Général Eisenhower, 75008 Paris; Palais de la Découverte, avenue Franklin-D-Roosevelt, 75008 Paris
☎ Galeries Nationales: 01 44 13 17 17; Palais Découverte: 01 56 43 20 21
🕐 Galeries Nationales: variable; Palais Découverte: 9:30–6, Sun 10–7; closed Mon
🍴 Café-bar (€)
Ⓜ Champs-Elysées-Clemenceau
🚌 28, 42, 49, 72, 73, 80, 83
♿ Galeries Nationales: excellent; Palais: none
👋 Galeries Nationales: variable; Palais Découverte: moderate

Built at the same time as the Pont Alexandre III for the 1900 World Exhibition, this enormous steel and glass structure, concealed behind stone walls, is typical of the *belle époque* style: Ionic columns line the imposing façade and colossal bronze statues decorate the four corners.

Major international art exhibitions – Tutankhamun, Renoir, Gauguin and Picasso, to name but a few – are traditionally held in the Galeries Nationales, on the Champs-Elysées side of the building.

The west part of the Grand Palais houses the Palais de la Découverte, inaugurated in 1937 to bring science within the grasp of the general public and keep them informed of the latest scientific developments. There are interactive experiments, documentary films and a planetarium. Recent additions are the Electrostatic exhibition and the Sun room.

Elaborate statues adorn the Grand Palais

The Passage des Panoramas shopping arcade in boulevard Montmartre

GRANDS BOULEVARDS ✪

These busy arteries, stretching from the place de la République to the Madeleine and lined with cinemas, theatres, cafés and shops, have today fallen victim to their long tradition of popular entertainment, choked by traffic jams and disfigured by aggressive neon signs, cheap snack bars and general neglect.

The 'boulevards' were laid out as a tree-lined promenade in the 17th century, when some of the city's medieval fortifications were demolished; two ceremonial arches, the Porte St-Martin and the Porte St-Denis, replaced the town gates.

The popularity of the boulevards peaked during the 19th century, with popular attractions in the east (theatre, dancing, circus and busking) and a more refined choice of entertainment in the west, especially after the building of the opera house. Several shopping arcades were also opened, including the Passage des Panoramas in boulevard Montmartre, opposite **Musée Grévin**, the famous waxworks museum, and at the end of the century, one of the first cinemas was inaugurated in boulevard St-Denis by the Lumière brothers.

Today, the boulevards still attract crowds of cinema- and theatre-goers but their general shabby appearance also encourages a rowdy element, particularly between the Porte St-Martin and the rue de Richelieu. Fortunately, complete renovation is underway.

Grands Boulevards
🛈 28C4
✉ From east to west: boulevards St-Martin, St-Denis, de Bonne Nouvelle, Poissonnière, Montmartre, des Italiens, des Capucines and de la Madeleine
🚇 République, Strasbourg-St-Denis, Bonne Nouvelle, Rue Montmartre, Richelieu-Drouot, Opéra, Madeleine

Musée Grévin
🛈 29D4
✉ 10 boulevard Montmartre, 75009 Paris
☎ 01 47 70 85 05
🕐 Mon–Fri 10–6.30; Sat–Sun 10–7
🍴 Near by along the boulevards (€–€€)
🚇 Rue Montmartre
🚌 20, 48, 74, 85
♿ None 💷 Expensive
❓ Shop

In the Know

If you only have a short time to visit Paris, or would like to get a real flavour of the city, here are some ideas:

10
Ways To Be A Local

Stand on the place Charles-de-Gaulle during the rush hour to get the feel of the Parisian pace of life.

Go into a crowded café at lunchtime and rub shoulders with hard-working Parisians.

Go to 'Les Champs' (Champs-Elysées) on Saturday night and meet Parisians enjoying themselves.

Soak in the atmosphere of old Paris along the Canal St-Martin.

Buy a baguette and some cheese in the rue Mouffetard for an outdoor lunch in the nearby square des Arènes de Lutèce.

Sample the village atmosphere in Le Marais on Sunday afternoon, together with thousands of Parisians.

Talk to the *bouquinistes* **along the Seine**, usually only too willing to comment on local news and people.

Mingle with Parisian youth along boulevard St-Germain.

Learn how to bargain at the Marché aux Puces, Porte de Clignancourt.

Don't talk to a Parisian about local driving.

10
Good Places To Have Lunch

Le Caveau du Palais (€€) ✉ 17 place Dauphine, 1st, ☎ 01 43 26 04 28; view of the lovely place Dauphine.

Brasserie de l'Ile Saint-Louis (€€) ✉ 55 quai de Bourbon, 4th, ☎ 01 43 54 02 59; *choucroute garnie.*

Le Polidor (€) ✉ 41 rue Monsieur-le-Prince, 6th, ☎ 01 43 26 95 34; French cuisine in the heart of the Latin Quarter.

La Victoire Suprême du Coeur (€€) ✉ 41 rue des Bourdonnais, 1st, ☎ 01 40 41 93 95; international vegetarian cuisine.

Georges (€€–€€€) ✉ Centre Pompidou (6th floor), 4th ☎ 01 44 78 47 99; fabulous views of Paris.

Le Toupary (€€) ✉ Samaritaine, 5th floor, 2 quai du Louvre, 1st, ☎ 01 40 41 29 29; panoramic view.

Bofinger (€€) ✉ 5 rue de la Bastille, 4th, ☎ 01 42 72 87 82; *belle époque* setting.

Restaurant du Palais-Royal (€€) ✉ 43 rue de Valois, 1st, ☎ 01 40 20 00 27; overlooking the Jardin du Palais-Royal.

A Priori Thé (€) ✉ 35–7 Galerie Vivienne, 2nd, ☎ 01 42 97 48 75; old-world surroundings.

Altitude 95 (€–€€) ✉ Tour Eiffel 1st floor, Champs de Mars, 7th, ☎ 01 45 55 20 04; brasserie with original airship décor.

Famous and Picturesque Cafés

• Café de la Paix, 12 boulevard des Capucines, 🚇 Opéra
• Fouquet's, 99 Champs-Elysées, 🚇 George V
• Café Marly, Le Louvre, 🚇 Palais-Royal
• Café de Flore, 172 boulevard St-Germain, 🚇 St-Germain-des-Prés
• Les Deux Magots, 6 place St-Germain-des-Prés, 🚇 St-Germain-des-Prés
• Le Procope, 13 rue de l'Ancienne-Comédie, 🚇 Odéon
• Café de la Mairie, 8 place St-Sulpice, 🚇 St-Sulpice
• Café Martini, 11 rue du Pas de la Mule, 🚇 Chemin-Vert
• La Closerie des Lilas, 171 boulevard du Montparnasse, 🚇 Vavin
• Le Sancerre, 35 rue des Abbesses, 🚇 Abbesses

10

Top Activities

Walking (pedestrian areas): footpath along the river; quartier Montorgueil north of Les Halles.
Cycle tours: Paris à Vélo, c'est Sympa! ✉ 22 rue Alphonse Baudin, 11th, ☎ 01 48 87 60 01.
Rowing on the lake in Bois de Boulogne.
Horse riding: Société d'Equitation de Paris, ☎ 01 45 01 20 06.
Theme parks: Disneyland Paris (➤ 81), Parc Astérix (➤ 85).
Parc Floral de Paris ✉ Bois de Vincennes, 12th; flowers, medicinal plants etc.
Aquaboulevard ✉ 4–6 rue Louis-Armand, 15th, ☎ 01 40 60 10 00; fun with water.
Hot-air ballooning: Montgolfières Aventures, ☎ 01 40 47 61 04.
Roller skating rallies: ☎ 01 44 54 07 44; held every Sun.
Leisure park: Base de Plein Air, ✉ St-Quentin-en-Yvelines, ☎ 01 30 62 20 12, RER C.

10

Bird's-Eye Views

• Tour Eiffel (➤ 25)
• Sacré-Coeur (➤ 70)
• Tour Montparnasse (➤ 62)
• Grande Arche de la Défense (➤ 18)
• Towers of Notre-Dame (➤ 22)
• Arc de Triomphe (➤ 32)
• Dôme of Les Invalides (➤ 19)
• Centre Georges Pompidou (6th floor, ➤ 16)
• Palais de Chaillot (➤ 40)
• Institut du Monde Arabe (➤ 54)

Forum des Halles

29D3

Rue Pierre Lescot, rue
Rambuteau, rue Berger,
75001 Paris

In the complex (€)

Les Halles

29, 38, 47

Lifts to all levels

LES HALLES

Paris's legendary food market has long gone from the centre of the capital, but the name is here to stay, tinged for many Parisians with a certain nostalgia, for when the 19th-century steel and glass 'pavillons de Baltard' were removed in 1969 and the noisy activity of the market suddenly stopped, the character of this popular district changed beyond recognition. A vast gaping hole was left between one of the most beautiful churches in Paris and a lovely Renaissance fountain. A commercial and cultural complex was built underground with a central patio surrounded by glass-roofed galleries that barely reach ground level. Above ground, a garden was laid over the remaining space, with a children's area and shaded walks and yet more graceful steel and glass structures.

The underground complex, spread over several levels, comprises shops, including a group of young fashion designers (Poste Berger, level −1), restaurants, an auditorium, a gymnasium and a swimming pool, as well as a tropical greenhouse.

A huge stone head leaning against a hand decorates the semicircular paved area in front of the Eglise St-Eustache. The latter was built over a period of a hundred years, in a blend of late Gothic, Renaissance and neo-classical styles. From the church, a path leads across the gardens to the square des Innocents and the beautiful Renaissance fountain, built and carved in the mid-16th century by Pierre Lescot and Jean Goujon, who also worked on the Louvre.

HISTOIRE NATURELLE, MUSÉE NATIONAL D'
(➤ 68)

HOMME, MUSÉE DE L'
(➤ 40)

Eglise St-Eustache, with the incongruous giant head and hand sculpture

*Place de l'Hôtel de Ville, formerly called place de Grève (*grève *is French for shore)*

Above: *the town hall clock*

HÔTEL DE VILLE ✪

The town hall of the city of Paris has been standing on this site since the 14th century. Destroyed by fire during the Paris Commune in 1871, it was rebuilt almost straight away in neo-Renaissance style. On the exterior are 136 statues representing famous historic figures.

Near by stands the 52m-high Tour St-Jacques, the only remaining part of a demolished church. In 1648, Pascal used the tower to verify his experiments on the weight of air. Later, a meteorological station was set up at the top and the tower became the property of the city of Paris.

On the east side of the town hall, the Eglise St-Gervais-St-Protais is a splendid example of a successful blend of Flamboyant Gothic and classical styles.

✚ 29E3
✉ Place de l'Hôtel de Ville, 75004 Paris
☎ 01 42 76 54 04
🕐 Guided tour by appointment only
Ⓜ Hôtel de Ville
🚌 38, 47, 58, 67, 70, 72, 74, 75, 96,
♿ Good
💰 Free

INSTITUT DE FRANCE ✪

The imposing classical building facing the Louvre across the river was commissioned by Cardinal Mazarin, as a school for provincial children, and designed by Le Vau; it is surmounted by a magnificent dome and houses the Institut de France, an institution created in 1795 to unite under one roof five prestigious academies, including the famous (and oldest) Académie Française founded in 1635 by Richelieu. It also houses the Bibliothèque Mazarine, Mazarin's own collection of rare editions.

✚ 29D3
✉ 23 quai de Conti, 75006 Paris
☎ 01 44 41 44 35
🕐 Sat, Sun guided tours by appointment only
Ⓜ Pont Neuf, Louvre, Odéon
🚌 24, 27, 39, 48, 58, 70, 95
♿ None   💰 Inexpensive

53

INSTITUT DU MONDE ARABE

The Institute of Arab and Islamic Civilisation is a remarkable piece of modern architecture designed by the French architect Jean Nouvel. Its glass and aluminium façade, reminiscent of a *musharabia* (carved wooden screen), discretely refers to Arab tradition. The seventh floor houses a museum of Islamic art and civilisation from the 8th century to the present day. The ninth floor offers a panoramic view of the Ile de la Cité and Ile St-Louis near by.

LES INVALIDES (► 19, TOP TEN)

JACQUEMART-ANDRÉ, MUSÉE ✪✪

This elegant 19th-century mansion, recently refurbished, houses the remarkable collections of European art bequeathed by the wealthy widow of a banker to the Institut de France. French 18th-century art includes paintings by Boucher, Chardin, Greuze and Watteau, as well as sculptures by Houdon and Pigalle, furniture, Beauvais tapestries and *objets d'art*. There are also 17th-century Dutch and Flemish masterpieces and an exceptionally fine collection of Italian Renaissance art including works by Mantegna, Donatello, Botticelli and Uccello.

JEU DE PAUME ✪

One of two pavilions built in the late 19th century at the entrance of the Jardin des Tuileries, the Jeu de Paume, on the rue de Rivoli side, was intended for the practice of a game similar to tennis. It later housed the national collection of Impressionist paintings until it was transferred to the Musée d'Orsay. Reopened in June 2004 after refurbishment, the Jeu de Paume is now exclusively devoted to the art of photography, holding thematic and monographic exhibitions from the 19th century to the 21st century.

Sidebar (Institut du Monde Arabe):

✚ 29E2
✉ 1 rue des Fossés St-Bernard, 75005 Paris
☎ 01 40 51 38 38
🕐 10–6; closed Mon, 1 May
🍴 Restaurant (€–€€)
Ⓜ Jussieu
🚌 24, 63, 67, 86, 87, 89
♿ Good 💳 Inexpensive
❓ Guided tours, shops

Sidebar (Jacquemart-André):

✚ 28B5
✉ 158 boulevard Haussmann, 75008 Paris
☎ 01 42 62 11 59
🕐 10–6
🍴 Tearoom (£)
Ⓜ Miromesnil, St-Philippe-du-Roule
🚌 22, 28, 43, 52, 80, 83, 84, 93
♿ None 💳 Moderate

Sidebar (Jeu de Paume):

✚ 28C4
✉ 1 place de la Concorde, 75001 Paris
☎ 01 47 03 12 52
🕐 Wed–Fri 12–7, Sat–Sun 10–7, Tue 12–9:30
🍴 Café (€) Ⓜ Concorde
🚌 24, 42, 52, 72, 73, 84, 94
♿ Very good 💳 Moderate
❓ Shop

Opposite page: *Eglise de la Madeleine, not instantly recognisable as a church*

Right: *home of Edouard Jacquemart and Nélie André's European art collection; the former owners' private apartments are also on show*

LE LOUVRE (▶ 20–1, TOP TEN)

MADELEINE, EGLISE DE LA ✪✪
Work started on this imposing neo-classical building in 1764, shortly after the completion of the place de la Concorde, but troubled times lay ahead and the partly constructed building was abandoned until 1806, when Napoleon decided to erect a temple to the glory of his 'Great Army'. He ran out of time to complete his ambitious project. It was then decided that the edifice would be a church after all and it was consecrated in 1845. The result is an impressive Graeco-Roman temple completely surrounded by tall Corinthian columns. Steps lead up to the entrance, which is surmounted by a monumental pediment. The interior is decorated with sculptures by Rude and Pradier; the magnificent organ was made by Cavaillé-Coll in 1846 and several well-known composers, including Camille Saint-Saëns, held the post of organist.

➕ 28C4
✉ Place de la Madeleine, 75008 Paris
☎ 01 44 51 69 00
🕐 7:30–7, Sun 7:30–1:30 and 3:30–7; bank hols variable
Ⓜ Madeleine
🚌 24, 42, 52, 84, 94
♿ None
💲 Free
❓ Shops

MAILLOL, MUSÉE ✪✪
This atttractive museum, situated in the rue de Grenelle next to a beautiful 18th-century fountain, is interesting on two accounts: it displays a great many works by the French painter and sculptor Aristide Maillol (1861–1944) as well as a private collection of works by Ingres, Cézanne, Dufy, Matisse, Bonnard, Degas, Picasso, Gauguin, Rodin, Kandinsky, Poliakoff etc.

Maillol's obsessive theme was the nude, upon which he conferred an allegorical meaning; he produced smooth rounded figures, some of which can be seen in the Jardin des Tuileries.

➕ 28C3
✉ 59–61 rue de Grenelle, 75007 Paris
☎ 01 42 22 59 58
🕐 11–6; closed Tue and bank hols
🍴 Cafeteria (€)
Ⓜ Rue du Bac
🚌 63, 68, 83, 84
♿ Good
💲 Moderate
❓ Shop

LE MARAIS

The sedate old-world atmosphere of this historic enclave at the heart of the city, its architectural beauty and cultural diversity are unique.

As its name suggests, Le Marais was once an area of marshland on the Right Bank of the Seine. In the 13th century, the area was drained and cultivated by monks and the Knights Templars. However, it was the construction of the place des Vosges at the beginning of the 17th century and the subsequent rapid urbanisation of the district that produced a wealth of beautiful domestic architecture and gave Le Marais its unique character. When fashions changed in the late 18th century, the district gradually became derelict and had to wait until the 1970s to be rediscovered and renovated.

Today Le Marais, which extends from the Hôtel de Ville to the place de la Bastille, offers visitors narrow picturesque streets, cafés and bistros, elegant mansions, tiny boutiques and a lively population that includes an important Jewish community. It is also one of the favourite haunts of the gay community.

Around every corner is another delightful mansion. These houses are no longer privately owned: some have been turned into museums, sometimes with striking results (Musée Picasso, ➤ 67). One of the most imposing, the Hôtel de Soubise, houses the **Musée de l'Histoire de France**, where historic documents are displayed amidst a profusion of Louis XV decoration. An unusual museum dedicated to hunting and nature (**Musée de la Chasse et de la Nature**) is housed in the Hôtel de Guénégaud des Brosses, built by François Mansart. Here hunting arms dating from prehistory until the 19th century are on display, plus paintings and decorative arts on the subject of hunting.

MARINE, MUSÉE DE LA (➤ 40)

Capturing the mansions, fountains and plane trees of the place des Vosges

Musée de l'Histoire de France

✚ 29E3

✉ Hôtel de Soubise, 60 rue des Francs-Bourgeois, 75003 Paris

☎ 01 40 27 60 96

🕐 Telephone in advance for opening times: restructuring taking place until spring 2005; temporary exhibitions

Ⓜ Hôtel de Ville

🚌 29, 75, 96   ⚙ None

💷 Inexpensive   ❓ Shop

Musée de la Chasse et de la Nature

✚ 29E3

✉ Hôtel de Guénégaud des Brosses, 60 rue des Archives, 75003 Paris

☎ 01 53 01 92 40

🕐 11–6; closed Mon and bank hols

Ⓜ Hôtel de Ville

🚌 29, 75

⚙ None   💷 Moderate

❓ Bookshop

A Walk Through Le Marais

Picturesque streets and carefully restored architectural gems make this an enjoyable walk.

Walk north from place de l'Hôtel de Ville along rue des Archives.

The Eglise des Billettes, on your right, has the last remaining medieval cloister in Paris.

Turn right into rue Ste-Croix de la Bretonnerie, then third left and first right.

Rue des Rosiers, at the heart of the Jewish quarter, is lined with a colourful array of traditional shops and restaurants.

Turn left into rue Pavée then left again.

Rue des Francs-Bourgeois is the liveliest street in the Marais, with unusual boutiques selling clothes, antiques and trinkets.

Turn right into rue du Temple.

The Musée d'Art et d'Histoire du Judaïsme, illustrates the history of Jewish communities from the Middle Ages to the 20th century.

Turn right into rue des Haudirettes and continue to the tiny place de Thorigny. The Musée Picasso (➤ 67) is on the left. Turn right, down rue Elzévir, past the Musée Cognacq-Jay (➤ 44) then left up the rue Payenne and right down rue Sévigné.

This is a delightfully peaceful area. Have a look inside the courtyard of the Hôtel Carnavalet (➤ 39).

Walk east to the end of rue des Francs-Bourgeois.

Soak in the unique atmosphere of the place des Vosges (➤ 75). Come out from the southern end.

Turn right in the rue St-Antoine. The walk ends in front of Eglise St-Paul-St-Louis.

Distance
3.8km

Time
2–4 hours depending on museum visits

Start point
Place de l'Hôtel de Ville
✚ 29E3
Ⓜ Hôtel de Ville

End point
Eglise St-Paul-St-Louis
✚ 29E3
Ⓜ St Paul

Lunch
Café Martini
✉ 11 rue du Pas-de-la-Mule, 4th
☎ 01 42 77 05 04

Fashionable though the area may be, long-established shops and businesses still survive in Le Marais

<table>
<tr><td>🕂</td><td>Off map 28A4</td></tr>
<tr><td>✉</td><td>2 rue Louis Boilly, 75016
Paris</td></tr>
<tr><td>☎</td><td>01 42 24 07 02</td></tr>
<tr><td>🕐</td><td>10–5:30; closed Mon, 1
May, 25 Dec</td></tr>
<tr><td>🍴</td><td>Cafés and restaurants
(€–€€) in nearby place de
la Muette</td></tr>
<tr><td>Ⓜ</td><td>La Muette</td></tr>
<tr><td>🚌</td><td>22, 32, 52, 63</td></tr>
<tr><td>♿</td><td>Good</td></tr>
<tr><td>💷</td><td>Moderate</td></tr>
<tr><td>❓</td><td>Shops</td></tr>
</table>

MARMOTTAN-MONET, MUSÉE ⭐⭐

Although situated off the beaten track, this gallery is a
must for anyone interested in the Impressionist movement
and in Monet in particular.

The museum was named after Paul Marmottan, who
bequeathed his house and his private collections of
Renaissance and 18th- and 19th-century art to the Institut
de France. These were later enriched by several bequests,
including 100 paintings by Monet donated by his son:
detailed studies of Monet's garden in Giverny, particularly
a group of *nymphéas* (water lilies) paintings, provide
insights into the artist's approach (see also Musée de
l'Orangerie, ➤ 64) and there are paintings of Rouen
Cathedral (done in different light conditions according to
the time of day) and of the River Thames in London. Most
important of all, perhaps, is a relatively early work, called
Impression, Soleil levant (1872), which created a sensation
at the time and gave its name to the Impressionist
movement.

There are also interesting works by Monet's contemporaries, Renoir, Pissarro, Sisley, Morisot and Gauguin.

<table>
<tr><td>🕂</td><td>Off map</td></tr>
<tr><td>✉</td><td>11 quai de Conti</td></tr>
<tr><td>☎</td><td>01 40 46 55 35</td></tr>
<tr><td>🕐</td><td>Tue–Fri 11–5.30, Sat–Sun
12–5.30</td></tr>
<tr><td>Ⓜ</td><td>Odéon, Pont-Neuf</td></tr>
<tr><td>🚌</td><td>24, 27, 39, 48, 58, 70, 95</td></tr>
<tr><td>♿</td><td>None</td></tr>
<tr><td>💷</td><td>Inexpensive</td></tr>
</table>

MONNAIE DE PARIS, MUSÉE DE LA ⭐

This museum devoted to the history of French currency is
housed in the Hôtel des Monnaies (the Mint), a fine 18th-
century building standing on the left bank, next to the
Institut de France. Coins, medals, paintings, sculptures,
historic documents, ancient tools and machinery illustrate
the evolution of minting in France from around 300BC to
the present. Note in particular the Ulhorn press dating from
1807. There are audiovisual presentations and a tour
specially tailored to children.

<table>
<tr><td>🕂</td><td>29D5</td></tr>
<tr><td>✉</td><td>75018 Paris</td></tr>
<tr><td>🍴</td><td>Several (€–€€€)</td></tr>
<tr><td>Ⓜ</td><td>Abbesses, Anvers,
Lamarck-Caulaincourt</td></tr>
<tr><td>🚌</td><td>Montmartrobus</td></tr>
</table>

Musée de Montmartre

<table>
<tr><td>✉</td><td>12 rue Cortot, 75018
Paris</td></tr>
<tr><td>☎</td><td>01 46 06 61 11</td></tr>
<tr><td>🕐</td><td>10–12.30, 1.30–6; closed
Mon, 1 Jan, 1 May,
25 Dec</td></tr>
<tr><td>♿</td><td>None 💷 Inexpensive</td></tr>
<tr><td>❓</td><td>Exhibitions, bookshop</td></tr>
</table>

MONTMARTRE ⭐⭐⭐

This unassuming village overlooking Paris became a myth
during the 19th century, when it was taken over by artists
and writers attracted by its picturesque surroundings and
Bohemian way of life. La 'Butte' (the mound) managed to
retain its village atmosphere and now that the area has
become a major tourist attraction, an undefinable nostalgia
lingers on, perpetuating Montmartre's magic appeal.

In its heyday, the district was the favourite haunt and
home of many famous artists. They met in cafés and in
cabarets such as the Moulin-Rouge (1889), whose singers
and dancers acquired world-wide fame through Toulouse-
Lautrec's paintings and posters. Halfway up the hill, a
wooden construction (13 place Emile-Goudeau) known as
the Bateau-Lavoir, where, amongst others, Picasso,

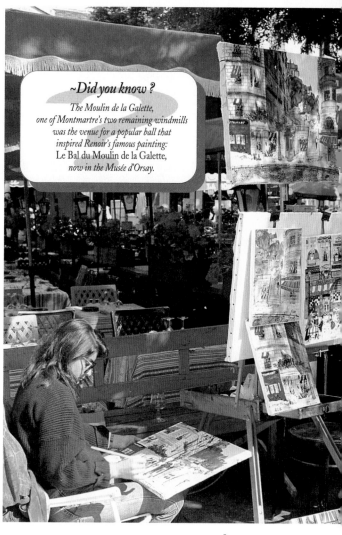

~Did you know ?

*The Moulin de la Galette,
one of Montmartre's two remaining windmills
was the venue for a popular ball that
inspired Renoir's famous painting:*
Le Bal du Moulin de la Galette,
now in the Musée d'Orsay.

Braque and Juan Gris had their studios, was the modest birthplace of Cubism; destroyed by fire in 1970, it has since been rebuilt. At the top of the hill stands the village square, place du Tertre, close to the Sacré-Coeur basilica (► 70). The **Musée de Montmartre** has works and memorabilia by the artists who lived here, and the narrow cobbled streets of the 'Butte' still have some amazing sights to offer, including a vineyard in the picturesque rue des Saules and two windmills in the twisting rue Lepic.

Today's artists follow in the footsteps of the famous 19th- and early 20th-century painters who made Montmartre their home

A Walk Through Montmartre

A walk through Montmartre is more like a pilgrimage. Allow 3 hours and time for the unexpected such as having your portrait done in place du Tertre!

Start from the square d'Anvers and walk north along rue de Stienkerque.

Facing you are the impressive steps leading to the Sacré-Coeur basilica. On the left, a funicular makes the climb easier.

Walk west along rue Tardieu to place des Abbesses.

This is the focal point of social life in Montmartre. Le Sancerre near by (if you can get in), is the most popular bar in the area. The métro entrance is in typical art nouveau style.

Continue northwest and turn right into rue Ravignan leading to place Emile–Goudeau.

The tiny square is one of the most authentic spots in Montmartre. The wooden Bateau-Lavoir, immortalised by Picasso, Braque and Gris, stood at No 13.

Continue up the winding street to rue Lepic then turn right towards the intersection of rue des Saules and rue St-Rustique.

The Auberge de la Bonne Franquette was the favourite haunt of the Impressionists, of Toulouse-Lautrec and Utrillo.

Rue Poulbot on the right leads to place du Calvaire (view), right round to place du Tertre.

The whole square is congested with easels and would-be artists. Go round the right side of the 12th-century Eglise St-Pierre to the Sacré-Coeur basilica (➤ 70).

Walk back to rue des Saules and follow it down to the other side of the hill.

At the corner of rue St-Vincent, watch out for the Montmartre vineyard and the Au Lapin Agile nightclub, the rendezvous of young artists and writers in the early 1900s.

Rue St-Vincent on the left leads to rue Caulaincourt where the walk ends.

Distance
2.2km

Time
3–4 hours

Start point
Square d'Anvers
🚇 29D5
🚉 Anvers

End point
Rue Caulaincourt
🚇 Off map 29D5
🚉 Lamarck-Caulaincourt

Lunch
Au Clair de la Lune
✉ 9 rue Poulbot
☎ 01 42 58 97 03

Opposite page:
Montmartre by night

61

Left: *rue de la Gaîté, Montparnasse*
Right: *the Musée de la Musique*

MONTPARNASSE ⭐⭐

Fashions change quickly in artistic circles and, soon after the turn of the century, young artists and writers left Montmartre to settle on the Left Bank, in an area which had been known as Montparnasse since medieval times. Modigliani, Chagall, Léger and many others found a home and a studio in La Ruche, the counterpart of the Bateau-Lavoir in Montmartre (► 59). They were later joined by Russian political refugees, musicians and, between the wars, American writers of the 'lost generation', among them Hemingway. They met in cafés along the boulevard Montparnasse, which have since become household names: La Closerie des Lilas, La Rotonde, Le Select, La Coupole and Le Dôme.

Since the 1960s the district has been systematically modernised and a new business complex built south of the boulevard. The 200m-high **Tour Montparnasse** stands in front of one of the busiest stations in Paris. The tower's 56th and 59th floors are open to the public and offer a restaurant and panoramic views. To the south-west, the circular place de Catalogne, surrounded by rows of glass columns, was designed by Ricardo Bofill.

🔲 28C1
✉ 75014 Paris
Ⓜ Montparnasse-Bienvenüe, Vavin

Tour Montparnasse
✉ rue de l'Arrivée, 75015 Paris
☎ 01 45 38 52 56
🕑 9:30AM–10:30PM (11:30PM in summer)
🍴 Le Ciel de Paris (€€)
♿ Good 👟 Moderate

MOYEN-AGE, MUSÉE NATIONAL DU ⭐⭐

This splendid museum of medieval art, also known as the Musée de Cluny, is housed in a 15th-century Gothic mansion – one of the last remaining examples of medieval domestic architecture in Paris.

The building stands at the heart of the Quartier Latin, on the site of Gallo-Roman baths dating from the 3rd century AD. The ruins are surrounded by a public garden. Inside the main courtyard, the elegant stair tower and corner turrets are particularly noteworthy.

The museum illustrates all the arts and crafts of the medieval period, the most famous exhibit being a set of tapestries known as 'La Dame à la Licorne', made in a Brussels workshop at the end of the 15th century. There is also an exceptionally fine collection of sculptures, including the heads of the kings of Judaea that decorated the façade of Notre-Dame Cathedral and were knocked down during the Revolution.

www.musee-moyenage.fr
🔲 29D2
✉ 6 place Paul Painlevé, 75005 Paris
☎ 01 53 73 78 00; 01 53 73 78 16
🕑 9:15–5:45; closed Tue, 1 Jan, 1 May, 25 Dec
🍴 In boulevard St-Michel near by (€–€€)
Ⓜ Cluny-La Sorbonne
🚌 21, 27, 38, 63, 85, 86, 87
♿ None
👟 Inexpensive
❓ Guided tours, shops, concerts

MUSIQUE, MUSÉE DE LA ✪✪

Housed within the vast Cité de la Musique (➤ 26), the museum presents a permanent exhibition consisting of some 900 musical instruments (out of a stock of around 4,500) dating from the Renaissance to the present day as well as a whole range of works of art and *objets d'art* inspired in some way by music. Temporary exhibitions are also organised in order to highlight the museum's collections, regular concerts and lectures and various cultural events take place in the 230-seat auditorium.

✚ Off map 29F5
✉ 221 avenue Jean-Jaurès, 75019 Paris
☎ 01 44 84 44 84
🕐 Tue–Sat 12–6, Sun 10–6; closed Mon
🚇 Porte de Pantin
🚌 75, 151, PC
♿ Very good 🏷 Moderate
❓ Guided tours, shops

NISSIM DE CAMONDO, MUSÉE ✪✪

This museum offers a delightful journey back into the 18th century.

In 1935, Count Moïse de Camondo bequeathed his private residence on the edge of the parc Monceau to the French nation in memory of his son Nissim, killed in action in 1917. The interior is arranged as an authentic 18th-century private home, including wall panelling, Aubusson and Savonnerie tapestries, paintings by Vigée-Lebrun and Hubert Robert, sculptures by Houdon and Sèvres and Chantilly porcelain.

✚ 28B5
✉ 63 rue de Monceau, 75008 Paris
☎ 01 53 89 06 50
🕐 10–5; closed Mon, Tue, 1 Jan, 14 Jul, 25 Dec
🚇 Villiers
🚌 84, 94
♿ None
🏷 Inexpensive
❓ Guided tours

NOTRE-DAME (➤ 22, TOP TEN)

63

28C4
✉ Place de l'Opéra, 75009 Paris
☎ 01 41 10 08 10
🕐 10–4:30; closed 1 Jan, 1 May and matinee performances
Ⓜ Opéra
🚌 20, 21, 22, 27, 29, 42, 52, 53, 56, 68, 81, 95
♿ None
💰 Moderate
❓ Guided tours at noon, shops

Above: the Opéra Garnier, epitome of late 19th-century ostentation

28C3
✉ Place de la Concorde, Jardin des Tuileries, 75001 Paris
☎ 01 42 61 30 82 (fax)
🕐 Closed for restructuring
Ⓜ Concorde
🚌 24, 42, 52, 72, 73, 84, 94
♿ Very good
💰 Moderate
❓ Guided tours, shops

OPÉRA GARNIER ☆☆

A night at the opera to see *Giselle* or *Sleeping Beauty* is one of the great moments of a visit to Paris, not only for the quality of the productions but also for the sheer splendour of what is still referred to as *the* opera, in spite of the fact that there are now two opera houses in Paris!

The Palais Garnier (named after its architect) was built in 1875 in neo-classical style, but the decoration is unmistakably late 19th century and includes a group of statues called *La Danse* by Carpeaux, a copy of the original now held in the Musée d'Orsay. Inside, the grand staircase and the foyer are magnificent. In the main hall, restored to its original splendour, visitors can now fully appreciate the ceiling decorated by Chagall.

The museum contains paintings, watercolours and pastels illustrating the history of opera and ballet from the 18th century to the present day, mainly through portraits of famous singers, dancers and composers.

ORANGERIE, MUSÉE NATIONAL DE L' ☆☆

The Orangerie houses the Walter-Guillaume Collection, consisting mainly of Impressionist and 20th-century paintings, and a set of monumental paintings offered by Monet to his country, representing the famous Nymphéas (water lilies, see also Musée Marmottan ➤ 58) in the artist's garden at Giverny. During the restructuring of the museum, a late-16th-century fortified wall, erected to protect the new Tuileries Palace commissioned by Catherine de Médicis, was discovered on the site. Reopening is scheduled for the beginning of 2006.

ORSAY, MUSÉE D' (➤ 23, TOP TEN)

PALAIS-ROYAL ✪✪

This is more than just another historic building, it is a pleasant, relatively peaceful area with the Jardin du Palais-Royal in its centre. Here, cultural institutions occupy a prominent place, next to charming arcades and picturesque old streets. The palace built by Richelieu and bequeathed to the king on the cardinal's death now houses the ministry of culture and two important constitutional bodies, but the gardens are accessible through archways situated all round. Enclosed by arcading on three sides and an elegant double colonnade along the fourth, they are a haven of peace, where Parisians working in the area love to window-shop during their lunch hour along the row of quaint little boutiques hidden under the arcades.

An 18th-century addition to the original building houses the Comédie-Française, France's National Theatre, where all the classics are performed. From the place André Malraux in front, the Opéra Garnier can be seen at the top of the avenue de l'Opéra.

To the east of the Palais-Royal, off the rue Croix des Petits Champs, the Galerie Véro-Dodat is one of several elegant arcades in the area. Further up the street, the place des Victoires, designed by Mansart in the 17th century, is worth a detour for its classical architecture and for its fashion boutiques.

➕ 29D4
✉ Place du Palais-Royal, 75001 Paris
🕐 Jardin: 8AM–11PM (midnight in summer)
🍴 In the gardens (€€)
Ⓜ Palais-Royal
♿ Jardin: free access

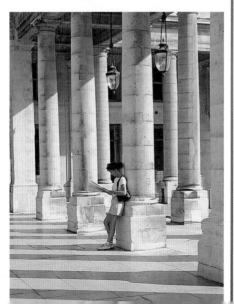

The peaceful arcades of the Palais-Royal (left) and (above) innovative sculpture in the main courtyard

29D2
Place du Panthéon, 75005 Paris
01 44 32 18 00
Apr–Sep 10–6:30; Oct–Mar 10–6; closed 1 Jan, 1 May, 25 Dec
Cardinal-Lemoine
84, 89
None
Moderate
Shops

PANTHÉON

Commissioned by Louis XV, the building was meant to replace St Genevieve's Church in the Quartier Latin; designed by Soufflot, who gave it the shape of a Greek cross surmounted by a high dome, it is now one of Paris's landmarks. Completed on the eve of the Revolution, it became a Pantheon for France's illustrious dead, among them Voltaire, Rousseau, Hugo, Zola, and more recently Jean Moulin (head of the French Resistance during World War II) and André Malraux (writer and highly successful Minister of Culture).

The domed Panthéon, imposing enough from a distance, but rather austere within

PARFUM, MUSÉE DU

The history of perfume from the time of the ancient Egyptians to the present is the fascinating subject of this museum, housed within the Fragonard perfumery, in two different places, both near the opera house.

PAVILLON DE L'ARSENAL

The late 19th-century iron and glass building houses an information centre devoted to Paris's urban planning and architecture throughout its troubled history. The permanent exhibition 'Paris, visite guidée' (Paris, a city in the making) shows the constant evolution of the cityscape by means of a dynamic, chronological display covering the ground, walls and ceiling of the main hall, with models, films, interactive terminals…a fascinating experience!

www.fragonard.com
28C4
9 rue Scribe, 75009 Paris; 39 boulevard des Capucines, 75002 Paris
Free

29E2
21 boulevard Morland, 75004 Paris
01 42 76 33 97
Tue–Sat 10:30–6:30, Sun 11–7; closed Mon
Sully-Morland 67, 86, 87
Good Free

PÈRE-LACHAISE, CIMETIÈRE DU ✪

Situated on the eastern edge of the city, the Cimetière du Père-Lachaise is Paris's most famous cemetery. The rising ground and abundant vegetation give the place a romantic atmosphere in spite of the great number of unsightly funeral monuments. Many famous people are buried here, including Musset, Chopin, Molière, Oscar Wilde, Delacroix, Balzac, even the unhappy lovers Héloïse and Abélard. In the south-east corner stands the Mur des Fédérés where the last 'communards' were shot in 1871.

+ Off map 29F4
⊠ Boulevard de Ménil-montant, 75020 Paris
☎ 01 55 25 82 10
🕐 Mon–Fri 8–6, Sat 8:30–6, Sun 9–6 (5:30 in winter)
🚇 Père-Lachaise
💷 Free
❓ Guided tours (in English) Sat 3 in summer

PICASSO, MUSÉE ✪✪✪

This is one of the most comprehensive museums devoted to the great 20th-century Spanish artist who lived and died in France. The collection was brought together after Picasso's death and consists of works donated to the State by his family in lieu of death duties, and his private collection – together totalling more than 200 paintings, sculptures, prints, drawings and ceramics.

The Hôtel Salé, situated at the heart of the historic Marais, was chosen to house this important collection. Like many other mansions in the area, it had been neglected and underwent extensive renovation to turn it into a museum. The interior decoration is very discreet, focusing attention on the beautiful stone staircase with its elegant wrought-iron banister.

Displayed in chronological order, the works illustrate the different phases of Picasso's artistic creation and the various techniques he used, from the blue period tainted with a certain pessimism (*Autoportrait bleu*), through the more optimistic pink period, to the successive Cubist periods. The tour of the museum is a fascinating journey in the company of one of the most forceful creative minds of this century. Picasso's private collection includes works by Renoir, Cézanne, Rousseau, Braque etc.

www.musee-picasso.fr
+ 29F3
⊠ Hôtel Salé, 5 rue de Thorigny, 75003 Paris
☎ 01 42 71 25 21
🕐 Apr–Sep 9:30–6 (5:30 Oct–Mar); closed Tue, 1 Jan, 25 Dec
🚇 St-Paul, Chemin Vert
🚌 29, 69, 75, 76, 93
♿ Very good
💷 Moderate
❓ Guided tours, shop

Above: *Picasso's Femmes à Leur Toilette (1938), from the museum*

🗺 29E2
✉ 57 rue Cuvier, 75005 Paris
☎ 01 40 79 30 00
🕐 Gardens: 7:30–sunset. Museum: 10–5; closed Tue. Zoo: 9–6
🍴 Cafeteria (€)
Ⓜ Jussieu
♿ Good
💰 Gardens: free; museum and zoo: moderate
❓ Lectures, exhibitions, workshops for children, shop

Jardin des Plantes

🗺 29D2

Sorbonne
✉ 47 rue des Ecoles and place de la Sorbonne (church), 75005 Paris
☎ 01 40 46 20 15
🕐 By appointment
Ⓜ Cluny-La Sorbonne
♿ None 💰 Moderate

St-Etienne-du-Mont
✉ Place Ste. Geneviève, 75005 Paris
🕐 9–7:30; closed lunchtime and Mon in Jul & Aug

PLANTES, JARDIN DES ✪✪

The botanical gardens owe their name to the 'royal garden of medicinal plants' created in the 17th century and extended by Buffon in the 18th century. Today they form the experimental gardens of the Musée National d'Histoire Naturelle (Natural History Museum) and make an ideal spot for a leisurely stroll; children love the ménagerie (zoo). There are also hothouses, an alpine garden and several exhibition halls, the most fascinating being the Grande Galerie de l'Evolution, illustrating the evolution of life on earth and Man's influence on it. Here, the display of endangered and extinct species is particularly interesting. Also featured are the scientists closely associated with evolution and the latest discoveries in the field of genetics.

LES QUAIS (▶ 24, TOP TEN)

QUARTIER LATIN ✪✪

This lively district remains to this day the undisputed kingdom of Parisian students. Situated on the Left Bank between the Carrefour de l'Odéon and the Jardin des Plantes, it was known in medieval times as the 'Montagne Ste-Geneviève' after the patron saint of Paris, and was later given the name of 'Quartier Latin' because Latin was spoken at the university until the late 18th century.

The **Sorbonne**, the most famous French university college, was founded in 1257; the present building dates from the late 19th century when well-known artists such as Puvis de Chavannes decorated the interior. The adjacent 17th-century church is a model of Jesuit style.

The **Church of St-Etienne-du-Mont**, dating from the late 15th century, combines Gothic Flamboyant and Renaissance styles.

A Walk Through the Quartier Latin & St-Germain-des-Prés

These lively Left Bank districts are the favourite haunt of Parisian youth.

Start at the crossroads of boulevard St-Germain and boulevard St-Michel.

Soak in the Left Bank atmosphere as you walk up the 'Boul Mich', a nickname used by generations of students. The small cafés on place de la Sorbonne are packed with students.

Take the next street on the left to reach the Church of St-Etienne-du-Mont (➤ 68).

It is well worth going inside to admire the Gothic chancel, Renaissance nave and magnificent rood screen.

Behind the church, follow rue Descartes to the right.

Beyond the charming place de la Contrescarpe lies the rue Mouffetard, known as 'la Mouffe', with its untidy shops and picturesque signs.

Go through the Passage des Postes (No 104) and turn right into rue Lhomond which leads back to boulevard St-Michel.

Stroll through the Jardin du Luxembourg past the beautiful Fontaine de Médicis. Come out by the west gate.

Walk down rue Bonaparte past place St-Sulpice and its superb fountain to boulevard St-Germain.

Near by are the picturesque rue de Furstenberg, rue Cardinale, rue de l'Echaudé and rue de Buci, with its lively market.

Rue St-André-des-Arts leads to the square of the same name with its quaint Fontaine Wallace. The walk ends here.

Distance
5km

Time
3–4 hours depending on stops

Start point
Crossroads of boulevard St-Germain and boulevard St-Michel
✚ 29D2
Ⓜ Cluny-La Sorbonne

End point
Place St-André-des-Arts
✚ 29D2
Ⓜ St-Michel

Lunch
Brasserie Lipp
✉ 151 boulevard St-Germain, 6th
☎ 01 45 48 53 91

Daily exercise in place St-Sulpice

69

www.musee-rodin.fr
- 28B3
- 77 rue de Varenne, 75007 Paris
- 01 44 18 61 10
- 9:30–4:45 (5:45 in summer, park 6:45); closed Mon, 1 Jan, 25 Dec
- Cafeteria (€)
- Varenne
- 69, 82, 87, 92
- Good
- Inexpensive
- Guided tours, shops

One of Rodin's most famous pieces, The Thinker

RODIN, MUSÉE ✪✪✪

One of the lovely mansions in the elegant Faubourg St-Germain, built by Gabriel in 1728, houses a unique collection of works by the sculptor Auguste Rodin (1840–1917). Rodin spent the last few years of his life in the Hôtel Biron as a guest of the French nation; when he died the collection of his works reverted to the State and the mansion was turned into a museum.

His forceful and highly original style brought him many disappointments and failures: his *Man with a Broken Nose* (now in the museum) was refused at the 1864 Salon and Rodin had to wait for another 15 years before his talent was fully acknowledged through his *St John the Baptist*. His major works are displayed inside the museum (*The Kiss, Man Walking*) and in the peaceful gardens (*The Thinker, The Burghers of Calais, The Gates of Hell*).

www.sacre-coeur-montmartre.com
- 29D5
- Place du Parvis du Sacré-Coeur, 75018 Paris
- 01 53 41 89 00
- Basilica: 7AM–11PM; dome and crypt: 9–6 (7 in summer)
- Abbesses (from here walk along rue Yvonne Le Tac, then take funicular or walk up steps)
- 30, 54, 80, 85, Montmartrobus
- Very good; access from the back of the basilica
- Basilica: free; dome and crypt: inexpensive
- Shops

Sacré-Coeur, among the city's most famous landmarks: the dome is the second highest point after La Tour Eiffel

SACRÉ-COEUR, BASILIQUE DU ✪✪

The white domes and campaniles of this neo-Byzantine basilica stand out against the Parisian skyline, high above the rooftops of the capital. Its construction at the top of Montmartre was undertaken as a sign of national reconciliation and hope after the bitter defeat suffered by France in the 1870 war against Prussia. Funds were raised by public subscription and work started in 1875, but the basilica took nearly 45 years to build and was inaugurated only in 1919, at the end of another war!

The view over Paris from the terrace in front of the building is breathtaking; an impressive number of steps leads down to the place St-Pierre; from the dome, an even more stunning panoramic view stretches for 50km around the city. The interior of the basilica is profusely decorated with mosaics.

ST-GERMAIN-DES-PRÉS ✪✪

The oldest church in Paris stands at the heart of the lively
Left Bank district of St-Germain-des-Prés. The Benedictine
Abbey of St-Germain-des-Prés, founded in the 6th century,
was throughout the Middle Ages so powerful a religious
and cultural centre that it became a town within the town.
It was completely destroyed during the Revolution; only
the church was spared. In spite of many alterations, the
church is a fine example of Romanesque style: the tower
dates from the 11th century as does the nave; note that
the carved capitals on the pillars are copies of the originals
kept in the Musée National du Moyen-Age (➤ 62). The
chancel and ambulatory date from the 12th century.

Facing the church is the Café des Deux Magots which,
like its neighbour the Café de Flore, was the favourite
haunt of intellectuals, in particular Sartre and Simone de
Beauvoir, immediately after World War II.

It is well worth exploring the old streets on the north
and east sides of the church and strolling along boulevard
St-Germain. The area between boulevard St-Germain and
the river and between the rue du Bac and the rue de Seine
is full of antique shops and art galleries.

➕ 28C3
✉ Place St-Germain-des-
   Prés, 75006 Paris
☎ 01 55 42 81 33
🕐 8–7
🍴 Cafés and restaurants
   near by (€–€€)
🚇 St-Germain-des-Prés
🎟 Free

*Despite unsympathetic
19th-century restoration,
the interior of the Church
of St-Germain-des-Prés
has retained its
Romanesque beauty*

71

29E2
75004 Paris
In rue St-Louis-en-l'Ile (€€)
Pont Marie
67, 86, 87

SAINT-LOUIS, ILE ✪✪

The peaceful atmosphere of this island is apparent as soon as you walk along its shaded embankment, lined with elegant private mansions that stand as silent witnesses of a bygone era. The island was formed at the beginning of the 17th century, when two small islands were united and joined to the mainland by a couple of bridges linked by the rue des Deux Ponts, which still exists; at the same time, private residences were built along the embankment and the straight narrow streets. The whole project was completed in a remarkably short time between 1627 and 1664. Since then, time seems to have stood still on the Ile Saint-Louis, which to this day retains its provincial character.

A few architectural gems can be seen along quai de Bourbon and quai d'Anjou, which offer fine views of the Right Bank. From the western tip of the island you can see Notre-Dame and the Ile de la Cité. Concerts are regularly given in the classical Church of St-Louis-en-l'Ile, richly decorated inside.

29D2
Place St-Sulpice, 75006 Paris
01 46 33 21 78
7:30–7:30
St-Sulpice
Free

ST-SULPICE, ÉGLISE ✪✪

The church and square of St-Sulpice form a harmonious architectural ensemble, mostly dating from the 18th century except for part of the church and the central fountain.

The original church, founded by the Abbey of St-Germain-des-Prés, was rebuilt and extended in the 17th century but was not completed until the mid-18th century. The Italian-style façade, designed by Servandoni, is surmounted by two slightly different towers crowned by balustrades and is in marked contrast to the rest of the building. Among the wealth of interior decoration are several statues by Bouchardon and outstanding murals by Delacroix (first chapel on the right) as well as a splendid organ by Cavaillé-Coll, traditionally played by the best organists in France.

Servandoni had also submitted plans for the square in front of the church, but they were abandoned and a monumental fountain designed by Visconti was eventually placed in its centre in 1844.

In place St-Sulpice, the Fontaine des Quatre Points Cardinaux features the busts of four respected churchmen. Although their figures face the four cardinal points of the compass, none of the men ever became cardinals!

Even without the support of flying buttresses, the soaring Gothic masterpiece of Sainte-Chapelle has stood the test of time

SAINTE-CHAPELLE ✪✪✪

The full splendour of this magnificent Gothic chapel can only be appreciated from inside, as Sainte-Chapelle is unfortunately closely surrounded by the Palais de Justice buildings. Commissioned by Saint-Louis to house the Crown of Thorns and a fragment of the true Cross, it was built in less than three years by Pierre de Montreuil (who also worked on Notre-Dame) and consecrated in 1248.

The building consists of two chapels, the lower one intended as a parish church for the palace staff and the upper one reserved for the royal family. The latter is a striking example of technical prowess: walls have been replaced by 15m-high stained-glass panels linked by slender pillars which also support the vaulting. The stained-glass windows, which cover an area of more than 600sq m, are mainly original and illustrate scenes from the Old and New Testaments.

LA TOUR EIFFEL (▶ 25, TOP TEN)

➕ 29D3
✉ 4 boulevard du Palais, 75001 Paris
☎ 01 53 40 60 97
🕐 10–5 (9:30–6 Apr–Sep); closed 1 Jan, 1 May, 1 Nov
Ⓜ Cité
🚌 96
♿ None
🖐 Moderate
❓ Shop

28C3
Rue de Rivoli, 75001
Paris
Apr–Sep: 7:30AM–8PM;
Oct–Mar: 7:30AM–7PM
Cafeterias (€)
Tuileries (access from rue
de Rivoli); Palais-Royal
(access from the Louvre)
24, 68, 72, 73, 84, 94
Free

TUILERIES, JARDIN DES ✪

This formal French-style garden was laid out by Le Nôtre in the 17th century, and was even then a popular public garden. The practice of hiring chairs goes back to the 18th century. The garden deteriorated over the years through extensive use and the increasing effects of pollution, but has now been entirely renovated as part of the Grand Louvre project. The stately central alleyway stretches in a straight line from the flower beds near the Arc de Triomphe du Carrousel to the place de la Concorde, where an octagonal ornamental pool is surrounded by various statues (the seasons, rivers) and flanked by terraces. On either side of the alleyway are groups of allegorical statues. There is a lovely view of the river and the gardens with the Louvre in the background from the Terrasse du Bord de l'Eau running along the riverbank.

The Tuileries, a popular place for whiling away a few hours, whether it be sailing model boats, strolling or sunbathing

28C4
75001 Paris
Opéra
72

VENDÔME, PLACE ✪✪

This square illustrates Louis XIV's style at its best, classical and elegant without being too emphatic. It was designed by Jules Hardouin-Mansart at the end of the 17th century and an equestrian statue of the King was placed in its centre. However, the statue was destroyed during the Revolution and in 1810 Napoleon had a tall bronze-clad column erected in its place, somewhat spoiling the architectural harmony created by the combination of arcades, pilasters and rows of dormer windows interrupted by the occasional pediment. In 1849, Frédéric Chopin died in No 12. Today the square is the headquarters of Paris's top jewellers.

A rather comical game of musical chairs went on for over 60 years to decide who should stand at the top of the column: Napoleon dressed as Caesar was replaced by Henri IV then by a huge *fleur de lys* before Napoleon reappeared...in less pompous attire, but not for long. A copy of the original statue commissioned by Napoleon III started another round; in 1871 the Commune took it down in anger but the Third Republic had it reinstated as a demonstration of tolerance...'much ado about nothing!'

VICTOR HUGO, MAISON DE (SEE BELOW)

LA VILLETTE (► 26, TOP TEN)

VOSGES, PLACE DES ✪✪✪

Totally unspoilt, this is Paris's oldest square and perhaps the loveliest for its moderate size, its discreet charm, its delightful brick and stone architecture and its peaceful central garden.

We owe this brilliant piece of town planning to 'Good King Henri' (Henri IV) whose initiative launched the development of Le Marais. The square is lined with identical pavilions over continuous arcading, dormer windows breaking up the monotony of the dark slate roofs; in the centre of the south and north sides stand two higher pavilions, known respectively as the Pavillon du Roi and Pavillon de la Reine. The square changed names during the Revolution and was finally called 'place des Vosges' in 1800 in honour of the first *département* to pay its taxes!

No 6, where Victor Hugo (1805–85) lived for 16 years, is now a museum (**Maison de Victor Hugo**), containing family mementoes, furniture, portraits, drawings by the writer himself as well as recon-structions of the various homes Hugo lived in.

Flat out in the place des Vosges: too much sightseeing?

✚ 29F3
✉ 75004 Paris
◉ St-Paul, Bastille, Chemin Vert
🚌 20, 65, 69, 76

Maison de Victor Hugo
✉ 6 place des Vosges
☎ 01 42 72 10 16
◉ 10–6, closed Mon and holidays
🍴 Restaurants near by
◉ Bastille
♿ None
🎟 Free
↔ Musée Carnavalet, place de la Bastille

75

St-Nom-La-Bretèche-Forêt-de-Marly *SNCF*
Versailles Rive Droite *SNCF*

Gabriel Péri (Asnières-Gennevilliers)
Bécon-Les-Bruyères *SNCF* 13

C1 Pontoise C3 Argenteuil *RER*

Saint-Denis Université 13

4 Porte de Clignancourt
RER D1 Orry La Ville Coye
Stade de France Saint-Denis

A1 St-Germain-en-Laye A3 Cergy-le-Haut A5 Poissy *RER*

1 Grande Arche de La Défense
3 Pont de Levallois-Bécon

Mairie de Clichy
Asnières-sur-Seine
Porte de Clichy
Clichy-Levallois
Brochant
La Fourche

Mairie de Saint Ouen
Garibaldi
Porte de St Ouen
Guy Môquet
Simplon
Marcadet-Poissonniers
Jules Joffrin
Lamarck
Abbesses
Château Rouge
Anvers (Sacré Cœur)

Esplanade de La Défense
Pont de Neuilly (Avenue de Madrid)
Les Sablons (Jardin d'Acclimatation)
Porte Maillot
Neuilly-Porte Maillot (Palais des Congrès)

Anatole France
Louise Michel
Porte de Champerret
Péreire-Levallois
Péreire (Maréchal Juin)
Rome
Wagram
Malesherbes
Monceau
Courcelles
Ternes

Place de Clichy
Pont-Cardinet
Liège
Blanche
Pigalle
St Georges
Notre-Dame-de-Lorette
Trinité (d'Estienne d'Orves)
Le Peletier
Cadet
Richelieu-Drouot
Grands Boulevards
Barbès-Rochechouart
Gare du Nord
Poissonnière
Bonne Nouvelle

Villiers 14 St-Lazare
E1 Haussmann St-Lazare
Havre-Caumartin
Opéra
Quatre Septembre
Bourse
Sentier
Châtelet-Les Halles

2 Porte Dauphine (Maréchal de Lattre de Tassigny)
Argentine
Victor Hugo
Avenue Foch
6 Charles de Gaulle Étoile
George V
Kléber
Boissière
Rue de la Pompe
Iéna
Miromesnil
St Philippe-du-Roule
Franklin D. Roosevelt
Champs-Elysées-Clemenceau
Alma-Marceau
Saint Augustin
Madeleine
Concorde
Auber
Pyramides
Palais Royal Musée du Louvre
Tuileries
Louvre-Rivoli
Pont-Neuf (La Monnaie)

Avenue Henri Martin
Boulainvilliers
La Muette
Passy
Trocadéro
Ranelagh
Jasmin
Avenue du Président Kennedy

Pont de l'Alma
Champ de Mars-Tour Eiffel
Bir-Hakeim (Grenelle)
Invalides
Assemblée Nationale
Solférino
SEINE
Musée d'Orsay
Rue du Bac
St-Michel
Mabillon
Odéon

10 Porte d'Auteuil
Michel Ange-Auteuil
Eglise d'Auteuil
Dupleix
La Tour Maubourg
Varenne
Ecole Militaire
St François Xavier
La Motte-Picquet-Grenelle
Vaneau
Sèvres-Babylone
Rennes
Duroc
Notre-Dame-des-Champs
St Germain-des-Prés
St Sulpice

Boulogne Jean Jaurès
Michel Ange-Molitor
Chardon-Lagache
Mirabeau
Javel André Citroën
Charles Michels
Avenue Emile Zola
Commerce
Cambronne
Ségur
Pasteur
Falguière
St Placide
Vavin
Raspail

10 Boulogne Pont de St Cloud (Rhin et Danube)
Exelmans
Porte de St-Cloud
Marcel Sembat
Boulevard Victor
Sèvres-Lecourbe
Félix Faure
Boucicaut
Lourmel
Volontaires
Vaugirard (Adolphe Chérioux)
Convention
Porte de Versailles
Corentin Celton
Montparnasse-Bienvenüe
Gaîté
Pernéty
Plaisance
Porte de Vanves
Edgar Quinet
Malakoff Plateau de Vanves

Pont de Sèvres 9
T2 Issy Val de Seine
Balard 8
Jacques-Henri Lartigue

Grande Arche de La Défense T2
Brimborion
Meudon sur-Seine
Les Moulineaux
Billancourt

C5 Versailles Rive Gauche (Palais de Versailles) C7 St-Quentin-en-Yvelines *RER*

12 Mairie d'Issy
Châtillon-Montrouge 13

© Communicarta Ltd, 2004   U.D.N.7c

B3 Aéroport-Charles de Gaulle 2-TGV
B5 Mitry-Claye RER

La Courneuve-8 Mai 1945 (7)

Bobigny-Pablo Picasso (5)

Pantin

Noisy-le-Sec

E2 Chelles-Gournay
E4 Tournan RER

(12) Porte de la Chapelle

Marx Dormoy

Aubervilliers-Pantin Quatre-Chemins
Porte de la Villette
Corentin Cariou
Crimée
Riquet

Porte de Pantin (Parc de la Villette)
Ourcq
Laumière
Danube

(7b) Pré St Gervais

Télégraphe

Porte des Lilas (3b)

Mairie des Lilas (11)

La Chapelle

Stalingrad

Jaurès

Bolivar
Botzaris

Place des Fêtes

St Fargeau

(3) Gallieni (Parc de Bagnolet)

Louis Blanc (7b)

Magenta

Château-Landon

Gare de l'Est (Verdun)

Château d'Eau

Strasbourg Saint-Denis

Réaumur Sébastopol

Étienne Marcel

Les Halles
Châtelet (11)

Colonel Fabien

Buttes Chaumont

Jacques Bonsergent

Goncourt (Hôpital Saint-Louis)

Belleville

Parmentier

Pyrénées

Jourdain

Couronnes

Ménilmontant

Père Lachaise

Pelleport

Porte de Bagnolet

(9) Mairie de Montreuil

Croix de Chavaux (Jacques Duclos)

Gambetta (3b)

Robespierre

Porte de Montreuil

République
Temple

Arts et Métiers

Filles du Calvaire

St Sébastien-Froissart

Rambuteau

Chemin Vert

Oberkampf

St Ambroise

Richard Lenoir

Voltaire (Léon Blum)

Charonne

Rue St Maur

Philippe Auguste

Alexandre Dumas

Maraîchers

Avron

Buzenval

Bréguet-Sabin

Rue des Boulets (Rue de Montreuil)

Saint-Paul (Le Marais)

Saint-Paul

Ledru Rollin

Faidherbe-Chaligny

Reuilly-Diderot

Nation (Place des Antilles)

Nation (2)(6)

Bastille

Hôtel de Ville

Porte de Vincennes

St Mandé-Tourelle

Chemin Vert

Château (Pont au Change)
Cité

St-Michel-Notre-Dame

Maubert-Mutualité

Cluny La Sorbonne

Pont Marie (Cité des Arts)

Sully-Morland

Gare de Lyon

Quai de la Rapée

(10) Gare d'Austerlitz

Montgallet

Jussieu

Dugommier

Picpus (Courteline)

Bel Air

Daumesnil (Félix Éboué)

Michel Bizot

Bérault

(1) Château de Vincennes

A2 Boissy St-Léger
A4 Marne-la-Vallée-Chessy (Disneyland® Resort Paris) RER

Cardinal Lemoine

Place Monge

St Marcel

Bercy

Cour St Émilion

Porte Dorée

Porte de Charenton

Liberté

Luxembourg

Censier-Daubenton

Campo Formio

Chevaleret

Quai de la Gare

Charenton-Ecoles (Place Aristide Briand)

LA MARNE

Port Royal

Denfert-Rochereau

Les Gobelins

Glacière
Corvisart

Nationale

(14) Bibliothèque François Mitterrand

Ecole Vétérinaire de Maisons-Alfort

Maisons-Alfort Alfortville

Maisons-Alfort Stade

St Jacques

Cité Universitaire

(4) Porte d'Orléans (Général Leclerc)

Gentilly

Mouton-Duvernet

Alésia

Tolbiac

Maison Blanche

Place d'Italie (5)

Olympiades

Porte de Choisy

Porte d'Ivry

Ivry-sur-Seine

Le Vert-de-Maisons

Maisons-Alfort Les Juilliottes

Créteil-l'Echat (Hôpital Henri Mondor)

Créteil Université

B2 Robinson
B4 St-Rémy les Chevreuse RER

Le Kremlin-Bicêtre

Villejuif-Léo Lagrange

Villejuif-Paul Vaillant-Couturier

(7) Villejuif-Louis Aragon RER

Porte d'Italie

Pierre Curie

(7) Mairie d'Ivry

C2 Massy Palaiseau
C4 Dourdan-la-Fôret
C6 St-Martin d'Etampes
C8 Versailles-Chantiers RER

D2 Melun
D4 Malesherbes RER

Créteil Préfecture (Hôtel de Ville) (8)

StylE45

authorised user Ref: 9C02117/ESP0604

Ile de France

'Ile de France', as the Paris region is called, means the heart of France; and this is exactly what it has always been and still is, the very core of the country, a prosperous and dynamic region, inhabited by one French person in five, with Paris in its centre. Roads, motorways and international railway lines converge on this central region, which has become one of Europe's main crossroads, with two major international airports.

Besides its tremendous vitality, the Ile de France offers visitors attractive natural assets, a rich cultural heritage and a gentle way of life. The countryside is domestic rather than spectacular, graced by picturesque villages, country inns, manor houses, historic castles, abbeys, cathedrals and beautiful parks and gardens.

> *'Here is the island shaded by poplars and Rousseau's grave...the castle by the still waters of the lake and the lawn which stretches like a savannah beneath the line of shadowy hills.'*
>
> GÉRARD DE NERVAL,
> *Sylvie* (new edition 1946,
> first published 1854)

———•———

Château de Dampierre

A Drive in the Painters' Footsteps

Distance
89km

Time
8–9 hours

Start point
Porte de Clichy

End point
Porte de la Chapelle

Lunch
Maison de Van Gogh
⊠ Place de la Mairie 95430
Auvers-sur-Oise
☎ 01 30 36 60 60

Musée Pissarro
⊠ 17 rue du Château,
95300 Pontoise
☎ 01 30 32 06 75
🕐 Wed–Sun 2–6; closed
bank hols

Maison de Van Gogh
⊠ Place de la Mairie 95430
Auvers-sur-Oise
🕐 10–6; closed Mon

Château d'Auvers-sur-Oise
⊠ Rue de Léry
☎ 01 34 48 48 50
🕐 Tue–Sun 10:30–4:30 (6,
Apr–Oct); last admission
1½ hours before closing
❓ Audio-visual show
recreating life at the time
of the Impressionists

Abbaye de Royaumont
⊠ 95270 Asnières-sur-Oise
☎ 01 30 35 59 00
🕐 10–6 Mar–Oct; 10–5:30
Nov–Feb

This drive takes you along the valley of the River Oise in the footsteps of the Impressionist painters who immortalised the little town of Auvers-sur-Oise.

Start from Porte de Clichy and drive north to Cergy-Pontoise (A15) and leave at exit 9 to Pontoise.

Camille Pissarro worked in Pontoise between 1872 and 1884; housed in a large house overlooking the river, the Musée Camille Pissarro contains works by the artist and some of his contemporaries.

Continue northeast along the D4 to Auvers-sur-Oise.

Several Impressionist painters settled here in the 1870s encouraged by Doctor Gachet, himself an amateur painter: Corot, Cézanne, Renoir and above all Van Gogh, whose painting of the village church has acquired world-wide fame. He died in the local inn, known as the Auberge Ravoux, and is buried in the cemetery, next to his brother Theo.

Cross the river and drive north along the D922 to L'Isle-Adam.

From the old bridge, there are lovely views of the river and its pleasure boats; on the way out towards Beaumont, have a look at the 18th-century Chinese folly, known as the Pavillon Cassan.

Follow the D922 to Viarmes and turn left on the D909 to the Abbaye de Royaumont.

Founded by St-Louis in 1228, this is the best preserved Cistercian abbey in the Ile de France.

Turn back. The D909 joins the N1 which takes you back to Porte de la Chapelle and the boulevard périphérique.

What to See in the Ile de France

CHANTILLY, CHÂTEAU DE ★★

Surrounded by a lake and beautiful gardens designed by Le Nôtre, the Château de Chantilly is one of the most attractive castles in the Paris region. It houses the Musée Condé, named after one of its most distinguished owners, Le Grand Condé. The 16th-century Petit Château contains the 'Princes' apartments' and a library full of precious illuminated manuscripts including *Les Très Riches Heures du Duc de Berry*, dating from the 15th century; the Grand Château, destroyed during the Revolution and rebuilt in Renaissance style at the end of the 19th century, houses a magnificent collection of paintings by Raphael, Clouet, Ingres, Corot, Delacroix, as well as porcelain and jewellery.

Facing the famous racecourse, the impressive 18th-century stables have been turned into a museum, the Musée Vivant du Cheval, illustrating the various crafts, jobs and sports connected with horses.

Chantilly – everything you could wish for in a château

- ✉ 40km north of Paris. BP 70243, 60631 Chantilly Cedex
- ☎ Château and Musée Conde: 03 44 62 62 62; Musée Vivant du Cheval: 03 44 57 40 40
- 🕐 Chateau: Mar–Oct 10–6, Nov–Feb 10:30–12:45, 2–5; closed Tue. Musée du Cheval: Mar–Oct 10:30–6:30; Nov–Feb 2–6
- 🍴 Near the station (€)
- 🚉 Gare du Nord to Chantilly-Gouvieux
- ♿ Moderate

Did you know ?

In 1671, while Louis XIV was visiting Chantilly at the invitation of Le Grand Condé, the most famous French chef, Vatel, killed himself because the fish he had ordered for the royal meal did not arrive on time!

DISNEYLAND RESORT PARIS ★★

The famous theme parks imported from the USA are now fully integrated into the French way of life and attracts an increasing number of families from all over Europe. They offer fantasy, humour, *joie de vivre*, excitement and the latest technological devices to ensure that your visit is a memorable one. Besides Disneyland Park and Walt Disney Studios, there is a whole range of 'typically' American hotels to tempt you to stay on for a day or two.

- ✉ 30km east of Paris. BP100 77777 Marne-la-Vallée
- ☎ UK: 08705 03 03 03; in France: 01 60 30 60 53
- 🕐 Varies with the season
- 🍴 Inside the park (€–€€€)
- 🚉 RER A Marne-la-Vallée/Chessy
- ♿ Good ♿ Moderate

ECOUEN, CHÂTEAU D' ⭐⭐

This elegant Renaissance castle dating from the first half of the 16th century is reminiscent of the famous castles of the Loire Valley; its painted fireplaces are especially noteworthy. It houses the Musée National de la Renaissance, whose collections of paintings, sculptures, enamels, tapestries, embroideries, ceramics, furniture, jewellery and stained glass illustrate the diversity of Renaissance art. Particularly fine is the 75m-long tapestry depicting David and Bathsheba's love story, made in a Brussels workshop at the beginning of the 16th century.

FONTAINEBLEAU, CHÂTEAU DE ⭐⭐⭐

As the name suggests, a fountain or spring, now in the Jardin Anglais, is at the origin of this splendid royal residence, which started out as a hunting pavilion at the heart of a vast forest. It was François I who made Fontainebleau into the beautiful palace it is today, although it was later remodelled by successive monarchs.

The imposing horseshoe staircase decorating the main façade was the scene of Napoleon I's moving farewell to his faithful guard in 1814 (see the Musée Napoléon I). Beyond this building lies the Etang des Carpes (carp pool) with a lovely pavilion in its centre, and further on the formal French gardens redesigned by Le Nôtre. The oldest part of the palace, including the keep of the medieval castle, surrounds the Cour Ovale.

The richly decorated State Apartments contain a remarkable collection of paintings, furniture and *objets d'art*, in addition to the fine coffered ceiling of the Salle de Bal and the frescoes in the Galerie François I.

<table>
<tr><td>✉</td><td>19km north of Paris. 95440 Ecouen</td></tr>
<tr><td>☎</td><td>01 34 38 38 50</td></tr>
<tr><td>🕐</td><td>9:45–12:30 and 2–5:15; closed Tue and holidays</td></tr>
<tr><td>🍴</td><td>In the château (€)</td></tr>
<tr><td>🚉</td><td>Gare du Nord to Ecouen-Ezanville, then 269 bus</td></tr>
<tr><td>♿</td><td>Very good</td></tr>
<tr><td>💷</td><td>Inexpensive</td></tr>
<tr><td>❓</td><td>Guided tours, shops</td></tr>
</table>

<table>
<tr><td>✉</td><td>65km southeast of Paris. 77300 Fontainebleau</td></tr>
<tr><td>☎</td><td>01 60 71 50 70</td></tr>
<tr><td>🕐</td><td>9:30–5 (6PM Jun–Sep). Closed Tue, 1 Jan, 1 May, 25 Dec</td></tr>
<tr><td>🍴</td><td>In the town nearby (€–€€€)</td></tr>
<tr><td>🚉</td><td>Gare de Lyon to Fontainebleau-Avon and 🚌 A or B</td></tr>
<tr><td>♿</td><td>Very good 💷 Moderate</td></tr>
<tr><td>❓</td><td>Guided tour, shops</td></tr>
</table>

Fontainbleau, a favourite retreat of royalty from the 16th century

A Drive In & Around the Forêt de Fontainebleau

The forest of Fontainebleau extends over a vast area along the left bank of the Seine, to the southeast of the capital.

Start at the Porte d'Orléans and follow the A6 motorway towards Evry and Lyon. Leave at the Fontainebleau exit and continue on the N37 for 7km; turn right to Barbizon.

This village gave its name to a group of landscape painters who settled there in the mid-19th century, among them Jean-François Millet. They were joined later by some of the future Impressionists: Renoir, Sisley and Monet.

The **Auberge Ganne**, which they decorated with their paintings, is now a museum.

Leave Barbizon towards Fontainebleau.

Take time to visit the castle (➤ 82), or at least the park, and to stroll around the town.

Drive southeast along the D58 for 4km bearing left at the Y-junction. Turn right onto the Route Ronde (D301).

This scenic route takes you through the forest and offers many possibilities for walking and cycling.

Turn left on the D409 to Milly-la-Forêt.

This small town nestling round an imposing covered market is a traditional centre for growing medicinal plants. The Cyclop (1km north) is a monumental modern sculpture which took 20 years to complete.

Follow the D372 for 3.5km and bear left for Courances.

The **Château de Courances** looks delightful, set like a jewel in a magnificent park designed by Le Nôtre, with pools, canals and small waterfalls.

Return to the main road and continue for 5km, then rejoin the motorway back to Paris.

Distance
143km

Time
7–9 hours depending on length of visits

Start/end point
Porte d'Orléans

Lunch
Le Caveau des Ducs
✉ 24 rue de Ferrare, 77300 Fontainebleau
☎ 01 64 22 05 05

Auberge Ganne
✉ 92 Grande Rue, 77630 Barbizon
☎ 01 60 66 22 27
🕐 Apr–Sep 10–12:30 and 2–6 (5 in winter), weekends 10–6 (5 in winter); closed Tue
💶 Moderate

Château de Courances
✉ 91240 Milly-la-Forêt
☎ 01 64 98 41 18
🕐 Apr–Oct: Sat, Sun and bank hols 2–6:30
💶 Moderate
❓ Guided tours

Barbizon's main street

✉ 25km west of Paris.
25 route du Mesnil,
78990 Elancourt
☎ 01 30 16 16 30
🕐 Apr–early Nov 10–6 (7 in
Jul and Aug); last
admission 1 hour before
closing
🍴 Two restaurants (€–€€)
🚇 Gare Montparnasse
♿ Good 🚌 Moderate
❓ Audio-visual show,
outdoor activities

FRANCE MINIATURE ✪

This open-air museum comprises a huge three dimen-
sional map of France on which 166 miniature historic
monuments have been arranged into a harmonious whole,
partly re-creating the atmosphere inherent to each place;
for instance the Château de Chenonceau reflected in the
calm waters of the Loire suggests the peaceful atmosphere of the Loire Valley. There are models of the Tour
Eiffel, the Sacré Coeur, the solitary Mont-St-Michel, the
pont du Gard and Gallo-Roman arenas, as well as many
beautiful castles, all made to a scale of 1:30. Here and
there, a typical French village focuses on ordinary daily life.

✉ 14km west of Paris.
Avenue du Château,
92500 Rueil-Malmaison
☎ 01 41 29 05 55
🕐 10–12:30, 1:30–5:15 (5:45
in summer); closed Tue,
1 Jan, 25 Dec. Bois-Préau
closed for renovation
🚇 RER Rueil-Malmaison
♿ Good
🚌 Inexpensive
❓ Guided tours, shop

*Château de Malmaison
with one of the garden
statues*

MALMAISON, CHÂTEAU DE ✪✪

The memory of Napoleon and his beloved Josephine
lingers on around 'La Malmaison' and the nearby Château
de Bois-Préau.

Josephine bought the 17th-century castle in 1799 and
had the wings and the veranda added. The couple spent
several happy years in Malmaison, and after their divorce
Josephine continued to live in it up until her death in 1814.
In the summer of 1815, Napoleon went to La Malmaison
once more before sailing for St-Helena. The castle then
passed through many hands before it was bought by a
banker, restored and donated to the State in 1904. It
contains various collections of 18th- and 19th-century
paintings (David, Greuze etc), porcelain and furniture.

The Château de Bois-Préau was offered to France by a
wealthy American, Edward Tuck, and now forms an
annexe to the collections in La Malmaison.

PARC ASTÉRIX ✪

This Gallic version of a made-in-USA theme park is based on the comic adventures of a friendly little Gaul named Astérix and his companions, who are determined to resist the Roman invaders. The story became famous worldwide through a series of more than 50 strip cartoons by Goscinny and Uderzo, which have since been translated into many languages.

Inside the park, visitors are invited to share Astérix's adventures as they wander through the Gauls' Village, the Roman City and Ancient Greece, travel on the impressive roller-coaster of the Great Lake and journey back and forth in time along the rue de Paris!

✉ 30km north of Paris.
BP 8, 60128 Plailly
☎ 03 44 62 34 04
🕐 Variable
🍴 Several choices (€–€€)
🚇 RER B3 from Châtelet or Gare du Nord to Roissy-Charles-de-Gaulle 1 then 🚌 Courriers Ile-de-France every half hour
♿ Excellent 👋 Moderate
❓ Gift shops, picnic areas, pushchair rental

SAINT-CLOUD, PARC DE ✪

This beautiful park, situated on the outskirts of Paris, extends over a vast hilly area overlooking the Seine. The castle designed by Jules-Hardouin Mansart for 'Monsieur', Louis XIV's brother, was destroyed by fire in 1870 and razed to the ground in 1891. It had been Bonaparte's favourite official residence when he was consul of the Republic.

The park was designed by Le Nôtre, who took advantage of the steep terrain to build a magnificent 'grande cascade', in which water flows gracefully from one pool to the next over a distance of 90m. At the top the site of the former castle is now a terrace offering lovely views of the capital. Near by is the Jardin du Trocadéro, an English-style garden with an ornamental pool and an aviary. There are many shaded alleyways offering delightful walks through the 460-ha park.

✉ 11km west of Paris.
92210 Saint-Cloud
☎ 01 41 12 02 90
🕐 7:30AM–8:50PM (7:50PM Nov–Feb, 9:50 May–Aug)
🍴 Cafés (€)
🚇 Pont de Saint-Cloud
👋 Free

Fun for all the family at Parc Astérisk

✉ 9km north of Paris.
1 rue de la Légion
d'Honneur, 93200 Saint-
Denis

☎ 01 48 09 83 54

◷ Winter: 10–5:15 (Sun
12–5:15); summer:
10–6:15 (Sun 12–6:15).
Closed 1 Jan, 1 May,
25 Dec

🚇 Saint-Denis Basilique

♿ None

💰 Moderate

❓ Guided tours

SAINT-DENIS, BASILIQUE ⭐⭐⭐

So many great architects and artists have contributed to make the Basilique St-Denis what it is today that the building is in itself a museum of French architecture and sculpture of the medieval and Renaissance periods.

An abbey was built on the site where St-Denis died following his martyrdom in Montmartre. Designed in the early 12th century by Abbot Suger, the nave and transept of the abbey church were completed in the 13th century by none other than Pierre de Montreuil, who also worked on Notre-Dame. It was for centuries the burial place of the kings and queens of France as well as of illustrious Frenchmen such as Du Guesclin. There is a wealth of recumbent figures and funeral monuments dating from the 12th to the 16th centuries, most of them the work of great artists: Beauneveu (Charles V, 14th century), Philibert Delorme (François I, 16th century), Germain Pilon (Catherine de Médicis, 16th century), Jean Bullant and Il Primaticcio (16th century). The basilica underwent restoration by Gabriel in the 18th century and again by Viollet-le-Duc in the 19th century.

✉ 23km west of Paris.

Château de Saint-Germain-en-Laye

✉ BP 3030, 78103 Saint-
Germain-en-Laye Cedex

☎ 01 39 10 13 00

◷ 9–5:15; closed Tue, some
bank hols

🚇 RER Saint-
Germain-en-Laye

♿ Very good

💰 Inexpensive

❓ Guided tours,
shops

SAINT-GERMAIN-EN-LAYE ⭐⭐

The historic city of Saint-Germain-en-Laye clusters round its royal castle, once the favourite residence of Louis XIV. François I commissioned the present Château Vieux (Old Castle) and retained Saint-Louis's chapel and the 14th-century square keep, now surmounted by a campanile. Le Nôtre later designed the gardens and the magnificent 2,400m-long Grande Terrasse. The Sun King stayed in

The Grand Terrace of the Château de Saint-Germain-en-Laye

Saint-Germain for many years and during that time private mansions were built around the castle for members of his court. When the court moved to Versailles in 1682, the castle was somewhat neglected but it was eventually restored by Napoleon III and turned into the Musée des Antiquités Nationales, which houses interesting archaeological collections illustrating life in France from earliest times to the Middle Ages.

SCEAUX, CHÂTEAU DE ✪✪

Very little remains of this castle, built for Colbert: the main entrance decorated with sculptures by Coysevox, the Orangerie to the left, the old stables opposite and the Pavillon de l'Aurore tucked away on the right. But the splendid park has been preserved: it is one of the most 'romantic' ever designed by Le Nôtre, with its tall trees reflected in the secluded octagonal pool, its peaceful Grand Canal and its impressive Grandes Cascades.

The castle, rebuilt in the 19th century, houses the Musée de l'Ile de France illustrating ancient regional arts and crafts and the history of castles in the Paris Region.

✉ 10km south of Paris. Château de Sceaux, 92330 Sceaux
☎ 01 41 87 29 50
🕐 Park: daily 8–sunset. Museum: 10–5 (6 in summer); closed Tue, 1 Jan, Easter, 1 May, 1 Nov, 11 Nov, 25 Dec
🍴 Cafeteria (€)
Ⓡ RER B Bourg-La-Reine
♿ Good
✋ Park: free. Museum: inexpensive
❓ Guided tours

A fine Sèvres urn at the porcelain museum

SÈVRES, MUSÉE NATIONAL DE LA CÉRAMIQUE DE ✪

The name of this Paris suburb was made famous by the porcelain factory transferred here in 1756 from its previous location in Vincennes. The unique 'Sèvres blue' ware, also known as 'lapis blue', became its trademark. The Musée National de la Céramique was founded at the beginning of the 19th century to house various collections of Sèvres and Saxe porcelain, Italian Renaissance ceramics, antique terracotta objects, glazed earthenware from the Far East and ceramics from elsewhere.

✉ 11km southwest of Paris. Place de la Manufacture, 92310 Sèvres
☎ 01 41 14 04 20
🕐 10–5; closed Tue, 1 Jan, Easter Mon, Whit Mon, 1 Nov, 25 Dec
Ⓜ Métro: Pont de Sèvres
♿ Good ✋ Inexpensive
❓ Guided tours

VAUX-LE-VICOMTE, CHÂTEAU DE ✪✪✪

This architectural gem, a 'little Versailles' built before Versailles was even designed, cost its owner, Nicolas Fouquet, his freedom and eventually his life – although much appreciated by the king for his competence in financial matters, he had dared to outdo his master! Fouquet, who had excellent taste, had commissioned the best artists of his time: Le Vau for the building, Le Brun for the decoration and Le Nôtre for the gardens. Louis XIV was invited to a dazzling reception given for the inauguration of the castle in 1661. The King did not take kindly to being outshone: Fouquet was arrested and spent the rest of his life in prison, while Louis XIV commissioned the same artists to build him an even more splendid castle, Versailles.

The castle stands on a terrace overlooking magnificent gardens featuring canals, pools and fountains; walking to the end of the terrace allows an overall view of the gardens and the castle. In the stables is a museum (Musée des Equipages) devoted to horse-drawn carriages.

✉ 51km southeast of Paris. Domaine de Vaux-le-Vicomte, 77950 Maincy
☎ 01 64 14 41 90
🕐 Mid-Mar to mid-Nov: Mon–Fri 10–1, 2–6, Sat, Sun 10–6. Candlelit visits: mid–May to mid–Oct Thu, Sat 8PM–midnight
🍴 Cafeteria (€)
Ⓖ Gare de Lyon to Melun then taxi
♿ None
✋ Expensive
❓ Shops

www.chateauversailles.fr

20km southwest of Paris.
78000 Versailles

01 30 83 78 00

Château: 9–5:30 (6:30 in
summer); closed Mon,
some bank hols.
Trianons: noon–5:30 (6:30
in summer); Parc: 7–5:30
(up to 9:30pm depending
on the season)
ceremonies

Cafeteria (€) and
restaurant (€€)

Gare St-Lazare to
Versailles Rive Droite

Good

Moderate

Guided tours, shops

VERSAILLES, CHÂTEAU DE ✪✪✪

The physical expression of a king's superego, Versailles
turned out to be one of the most splendid castles in the
world through the genius of the artists who built and
decorated it. What began as a modest hunting lodge
became the seat of government and political centre of
France for over a hundred years. A town grew up around
the castle to accommodate the court. Several thousand
men worked on the castle for 50 years, thousands of trees
were transplanted, and 3,000 people could live in it.

The castle is huge (680m long) and it is impossible to
see everything in the course of one visit. Aim for the first
floor where the State Apartments are, including the
famous Galerie des Glaces, as well as the Official
Apartments and the Private Apartments of the royal
couple, situated on either side of the marble courtyard. The
north wing contains the two-storey Chapelle St-Louis built
by Mansart and the Opéra, added later, by Gabriel.

The focal point of the park is the Bassin d'Apollon, a

Versailles: the south wing
(left) and the Apollo Basin
(above)

Below: *Château de
Vincennes*

magnificent ornamental pool with a bronze sculpture in its
centre representing Apollo's chariot coming out of the
water. Two smaller castles, Le Grand Trianon and Le Petit
Trianon, are also worth a visit, and Le Hameau, Marie-
Antoinette's retreat, offers a delightful contrast.

VINCENNES, CHÂTEAU DE ○○

This austere castle, situated on the eastern outskirts of
Paris, was a royal residence from the Middle Ages to the
mid-17th century. Inside the defensive wall, there are in
fact two castles: the 50m-high keep (currently undergoing
repair) built in the 14th century, which later held political
prisoners, philosophers, soldiers, ministers and
churchmen; and the two classical pavilions built by Le Vau
for Cardinal Mazarin in 1652, Le Pavillon de la Reine,
where Anne d'Autriche, mother of Louis XIV lived, and Le
Pavillon du Roi, where Mazarin died in 1661. The Chapelle
Royale, started by Saint-Louis and completed by François I,
stands in the main courtyard.

✉ 6km east of Paris.
Avenue de Paris, 94300
Vincennes
☎ 01 48 08 31 20
🕐 10–noon, 1–5 (6 in
summer); closed 1 Jan, 1
May, 1 Nov, 11 Nov, 25
Dec
🚇 Métro: Porte de
Vincennes
♿ None
💷 Inexpensive
❓ Guided tours, shops

A Drive Through the Vallée de Chevreuse

This drive will take you through the wooded Vallée de Chevreuse to Rambouillet, its castle and its park.

From the Porte de Saint-Cloud, follow signs for Chartres/Orléans. After 17km, leave for Saclay and take the N306 towards Chevreuse.

The little town of Chevreuse is dominated by the ruins of its medieval castle, which houses the Maison du Parc Naturel Régional de la Haute Vallée de Chevreuse (Natural Regional Park Information Centre).

From Chevreuse, drive southwest on the D906 to Rambouillet.

The 14th-century fortress is now an official residence of the presidents of the Republic. In the park, criss-crossed by canals, look for the Laiterie de la Reine (Marie-Antoinette's dairy).

Distance
93km

Time
7–9 hours depending on visits

Start/end point
Porte de Saint-Cloud

Lunch
Cheval Rouge
✉ 78 rue Général de Gaulle, 78120 Rambouillet
☎ 01 30 88 80 61

Maison du Parc, Chevreuse
www.parc-naturel.
chevreuse.org
☎ 01 30 52 09 09
🕐 Weekdays 10–12 and 2–6

Château de Rambouillet
☎ 01 34 83 00 25

Château de Dampierre
☎ 01 30 52 53 24

Musée National des Granges de Port-Royal
☎ 01 30 43 73 05

Drive back on the D906 for 10km and turn left on the D91 towards Dampierre.

The 16th-century stone and brick Château de Dampierre was remodelled by Jules Hardouin-Mansart for Colbert's son-in-law and still belongs to the de Luynes family.

Continue on the D91 across the River Yvette, negotiating the picturesque '17 bends' to the ruined Abbaye de Port-Royal-des-Champs (parking on left-hand side of the road).

During the 17th century, this former Cistercian abbey was at the centre of a religious battle between Jesuits and Jansenists. The Musée National des Granges de Port-Royal is in the park.

Continue along the D91 to Versailles and return to the Porte de Saint-Cloud by the Route de Paris (D10).

Above: *statue in the parkland of Château de Rambouillet*

Where To...

Above: *at the Jardin des Tuileries*

Paris

Prices
Prices for a three-course meal vary from around 15 euros to over 200 euros; the average price for each restaurant listed is shown by the pound symbol:

€ = budget (up to €30)

€€ = moderate (€30–75)

€€€ = expensive to luxury (over €75)

Nowhere is the saying 'Variety is the spice of life' truer than in Paris, for the city with a well-deserved reputation of being the gastronomic capital of the West has such a wide choice of eating establishments that selecting one can prove a hard task, even for Parisians. In Paris, the reality behind the word 'restaurant' is particularly complex since you can eat a three-course meal for as little as 10 euros in one of the local bistros, their red and white chequer-board tablecloths having become emblems of Parisian life, or for more than 200 euros in one of the temples of *haute cuisine*.

In between, there is an amazing array of cafés serving the inevitable *steak-frites* and *jambon-beurre* sandwiches, of *brasseries* with splendid late 19th-century settings, of chain restaurants marrying constant quality with a definite French touch, of wine bars and seafood places, of regional restaurants proudly reminding gourmets that French gastronomy is not the prerogative of Parisian chefs, and of cosmopolitan restaurants specialising in African, Lebanese or Vietnamese cuisine – to name but a few – and in Tex-Mex fare, increasingly popular with young French crowds.

Bistros are traditionally versatile and a great favourite of Parisians and visitors alike. Up to now, their ambitions had remained modest. However, in recent years, a new generation of bistros has emerged on the Paris scene: the famous chefs of

several exclusive restaurants have opened up-market bistros serving *haute cuisine* in less formal surroundings and at more affordable prices. Needless to say that these new bistros are very much in fashion: such is the case of La Régalade (► 97) and l'Epi Dupin (► 96), both on the Left Bank, where young chefs Yves Camdeborde and François Pasteau regale enthusiastic customers.

Right Bank Restaurants

L'Alsace (€€)
Alsatian specialities and seafood; terrace in summer.
✉ 39 avenue des Champs-Elysées, 75008 Paris ☎ 01 53 93 97 00 🕐 24 hours
🚇 Franklin-D Roosevelt

Les Amognes (€€)
Bistro serving imaginative cuisine in a relaxed atmosphere.
✉ 243 rue du Faubourg St-Antoine, 75011 Paris ☎ 01 43 72 73 05 🕐 Lunch, dinner; closed Sat and Mon lunch, Sun and 10–31 Aug 🚇 Faidherbe Chaligy

Bar à Huîtres (€–€€)
Fashionable seafood brasserie.
✉ 33 boulevard Beaumarchais, 75003 Paris ☎ 01 48 87 98 92 🕐 Lunch, dinner, open until 2AM
🚇 Bastille

Beauvilliers (€€–€€€)
Gourmet cuisine served in an elegant Napoleon III setting; terrace in summer.
✉ 52 rue Lamarck, 75018 Paris ☎ 01 42 54 54 42 🕐 Lunch, dinner; closed Mon lunch, Sun
🚇 Lamarck Caulaincourt

Bistro de Gala (€€)
In the 'Grands Boulevards' area, serving traditional French cuisine.
✉ 45 rue du Faubourg Montmartre, 75009 Paris ☎ 01 40 22 90 50 🕐 Lunch, dinner; closed Sat lunch, Sun and 2 weeks in Aug 🚇 Le Peletier

Blue Elephant (€€)
Thai cuisine in appropriate setting near Bastille. Try the *chiang rai*.
✉ 43 rue de la Roquette, 75011 Paris ☎ 01 47 00 42 00 🕐 Lunch, dinner; closed Sat lunch 🚇 Voltaire

Bon (€€)
Trendy restaurant; some vegetarian dishes.
✉ 25 rue de la Pompe, 75016 Paris ☎ 01 40 72 70 00 🕐 Lunch, dinner 🚇 La Muette

Brasserie Flo (€–€€)
1900-style Alsatian inn specialising in *choucroute* (sauerkraut) and seafood.
✉ 7 Cour des Petites Ecuries, 75010 Paris ☎ 01 47 70 13 59 🕐 Lunch, dinner 🚇 Château d'Eau

La Butte Chaillot (€€)
Refined cuisine served in a striking contemporary setting.
✉ 110 bis avenue Kléber, 75016 Paris ☎ 01 47 27 88 88 🕐 Lunch, dinner; closed Sat lunch and 2 weeks Aug 🚇 Trocadéro

Caveau François Villon (€)
Charming bistro located in 15th-century cellars. Live music is played at night.
✉ 64 rue de l'Arbre Sec, 75001 Paris ☎ 01 42 36 10 92 🕐 Lunch, dinner; closed Mon and Sat lunch, Sun 🚇 Louvre-Rivoli

Chez Clément Élysées (€)
Home style cooking.
✉ 123 avenue des Champs-Élysées, 75008 Paris ☎ 01 40 73 87 00 🕐 Lunch, dinner 🚇 Charles de Gaulle-Étoile

Chez Madame Vong (€)
Chinese and Vietnamese cuisine.
✉ 10 rue de la Grande Truanderie, 75001 Paris ☎ 01 42 97 49 07 🕐 Lunch, dinner; closed Sat and Sun lunch 🚇 Les Halles

Le Dôme du Marais (€€)
Imaginative cuisine based on fresh seasonal produce; historic surroundings.
✉ 53 bis rue des Francs-Bourgeois, 75004 Paris ☎ 01 42 74 54 17 🕐 Lunch, dinner; closed Sun 🚇 Hôtel de Ville

Le Dos de la Baleine (€)
Typical marais restaurant with undressed-stone walls; innovative cuisine.
✉ 40 rue des Blancs-Manteaux, 75004 Paris ☎ 01 42 72 38 98 🕐 Lunch, dinner; closed Sat lunch and Mon 🚇 Rambuteau

L'Etrier (€–€€)
Traditional French cuisine; good value. Reserve a table in advance.
✉ 154 rue Lamarck, 75018 Paris ☎ 01 42 29 14 01 🕐 Lunch, dinner; closed Mon, Sun and Aug 🚇 Guy Môquet

Grand Véfour (€€€)
Haute cuisine, surroundings of 18th-century décor; beautiful view of the Jardin du Palais-Royal.
✉ 17 rue de Beaujolais, 75001 Paris ☎ 01 42 96 56 27 🕐 Lunch, dinner; closed Fri night, Sat, Sun and Aug 🚇 Palais-Royal

How to Get The Best Value for Money
Whenever possible, choose one of the fixed *menus* rather than à la carte. Also note that *menus* are cheaper at lunchtime and that, unless otherwise specified, service is included in the prices quoted. Wines are generally expensive but house wines are often worth trying and are more reasonably priced.

Les Halles Tradition
In the days when the Paris food market was situated where the Forum des Halles now stands, there were many restaurants in the vicinity, such as Au Pied de Cochon, which served pig's trotters and onion soup to workers kept busy throughout the night. It later became fashionable for people out on the town to end up in one of those places in the early hours of the morning.

Les Grandes Marches (€–€€)
Seafood brasserie overlooking place de la Bastille.
✉ 6 place de la Bastille, 75012 Paris ☎ 01 43 42 90 32
🕐 Lunch, dinner 🚇 Bastille

Le Jardin (€€€)
Mediterranean-style *haute cuisine*; speciality: lobster roasted with spices.
✉ Hôtel Royal Monceau, 37 avenue Hoche, 75008 Paris ☎ 01 42 99 98 70 🕐 Lunch, dinner; closed Sat, Sun and bank hols 🚇 Charles de Gaulle-Etoile

Jipangue (€–€€)
Excellent Japanese cuisine.
✉ 96 rue La Boétie, 75008 Paris ☎ 01 45 63 77 00 🕐 Lunch, dinner; closed Sat lunch and Sun 🚇 St-Philipe-du-Roule

Lucas Carton (€€€)
Haute cuisine with authentic late 19th-century décor by Majorelle; good roast duck.
✉ 9 place de la Madeleine, 75008 Paris ☎ 01 42 65 22 90 🕐 Lunch, dinner; closed Sat lunch, Sun, Aug and Christmas 🚇 Madeleine

Nos Ancêtres les Gaulois (€€)
Convivial atmosphere; menu includes as much wine as you can drink.
✉ 39 rue St-Louis-en-l'Ile, 75004 Paris ☎ 01 46 33 66 07 🕐 Dinner only, lunch on Sun 🚇 Pont-Marie

Pavillon Puebla (€€–€€€)
In the lovely parc des Buttes Chaumont; elegant Napoleon III décor; speciality: lobster *à la catalane*.
✉ Parc des Buttes Chaumont (entrance on the corner of avenue Bolivar and rue Botzaris), 75019 Paris ☎ 01 42 08 92 62 🕐 Lunch, dinner; closed Sun, Mon 🚇 Buttes Chaumont

Le Piano des saisons (€)
Attractive new restaurant; seafood cuisine from south-west France.
✉ 11 rue Treilhard, 75008 Paris ☎ 01 45 61 09 46 🕐 Lunch, dinner; closed Sat–Sun 🚇 Miromesnil; St-Augustin

Piccolo Teatro (€)
Refreshing and inspired vegetarian dishes. Try the excellent soups.
✉ 6 rue des Ecouffes, 75004 Paris ☎ 01 42 72 17 79 🕐 Lunch, dinner; closed Mon, Christmas 🚇 St-Paul

Au Pied de Cochon (€€)
Traditional 'Les Halles' restaurant; try the pig's trotters and onion soup.
✉ 6 rue Coquillère, 75001 Paris ☎ 01 40 13 77 00 🕐 24 hours 🚇 Châtelet Les Halles

La Poule au Pot (€€)
A bistro maintaining the traditions of Les Halles.
✉ 9 rue Vauvilliers, 75001 Paris ☎ 01 42 36 32 96 🕐 Dinner; open until 6AM; closed Mon 🚇 Louvre Rivoli

Le Rouge Gorge (€€)
Charming wine bar with lots of atmosphere.
✉ 8 rue St-Paul, 75004 Paris ☎ 01 48 04 75 89 🕐 Lunch, dinner; closed Sun dinner 🚇 St-Paul

Stresa (€€)
Trendy Italian restaurant; booking advisable.
✉ 7 rue de Chambiges, 75008 Paris ☎ 01 47 23 51 62 🕐 Lunch, dinner; closed Sat dinner, Sun, Aug and Christmas 🚇 Alma-Marceau

Terminus Nord (€€)
A 1920s-style brasserie near the Gare du Nord; speciality: duck's *foie gras* with apple and raisins, seafood.
✉ 23 rue de Dunkerque, 75010 Paris ☎ 01 42 85 05 15
🍽 Lunch, dinner 🚇 Gare du Nord

Timgad (€€€)
Spectacular Moorish interior, innovative, exciting food and attentive service at one of France's best known Arab restaurants.
✉ 21 rue Brunel, 75017
☎ 01 45 74 23 70 🍽 Daily
🚇 Argentine

Train Bleu (€€)
Brasserie with late 19th-century décor illustrating the journey from Paris to the Mediterranean.
✉ Place Louis Armand, Gare de Lyon, 75012 Paris ☎ 01 43 43 09 06 🍽 Lunch, dinner
🚇 Gare de Lyon

Le Viaduc Café (€€)
Trendy bistro in the new Viaduc des Arts complex of workshops near Bastille.
✉ 43 avenue Daumesnil, 75012 Paris ☎ 01 44 74 70 70
🍽 Lunch, dinner 🚇 Bastille

Le Vieux Bistrot (€€)
Facing the north side of Notre-Dame; traditional French cooking.
✉ 14 rue du Cloître-Notre-Dame, 75004 Paris ☎ 01 43 54 18 95 🍽 Lunch, dinner
🚇 Cité

Wally el Saharien (€€)
This restaurant serves North African specialities with mountains of couscous.
✉ 36 rue Rodier, 75009 Paris
☎ 01 42 85 51 90 🍽 Closed Mon, Sun 🚇 Anvers

Left Bank Restaurants

Le Bamboche (€€)
Typical fish dishes from Provence.
✉ 15 rue de Babylone, 75007 Paris ☎ 01 45 49 14 40
🍽 Lunch, dinner; closed Sat lunch and Sun 🚇 Sèvres-Babylone

Bistrot du 7e (€)
Charming bistro near les Invalides, excellent value for money.
✉ 56 boulevard de la Tour-Maubourg, 75007 Paris ☎ 01 45 51 93 08 🍽 Lunch, dinner; closed for lunch Sat–Sun
🚇 Invalides, La Tour-Maubourg

Les Bookinistes (€€)
Fashionable restaurant along the embankment; up-and-coming young chef has made *nouvelle cuisine* into an art.
✉ 53 quai des Grands-Augustins, 75006 Paris
☎ 01 43 25 45 94 🍽 Lunch, dinner; closed Sat lunch, Sun
🚇 Saint-Michel

Brasserie Balzar (€€)
Popular smart brasserie close to the Sorbonne, serving good French dishes.
✉ 49 rue des Écoles, 75005 Paris ☎ 01 43 54 13 67
🍽 Daily 🚇 Cluny-La Sorbonne

Brasserie Lipp (€€)
Founded in 1880, this restaurant is always popular with the famous.
✉ 151 boulevard St-Germain, 75006 ☎ 01 45 48 53 91 🍽 Daily 🚇 St-Germain-des-Prés

Le Ciel de Paris (€€–€€€)
On the 56th floor of the Tour

Fast Food and Brunch
When the first McDonald's opened in Paris, most people thought it would be a flop! Well, fast food has become part of the French way of life and now the mecca of gastronomy has adopted another Anglo-Saxon habit – the brunch. More and more bistros in central Paris now specialise in this 'new' kind of meal, definitely 'in'.

French and Cosmopolitan Cuisine

Most restaurants selected here serve traditional French regional cuisine or what is loosely called *nouvelle cuisine*, as Paris's top chefs innovate in an effort to adapt to changing tastes and eating habits. There is a new emphasis on fish and seafood and it is now possible to enjoy a gastronomic meal without meat! There is also a strong tradition of world cuisine, essentially Italian, North African, Vietnamese, and Japanese.

Montparnasse; live music from 9PM.

✉ **Tour Montparnasse, 33 avenue du Maine, 75015 Paris** ☎ **01 40 64 77 64** 🕐 **Lunch, dinner** Ⓜ **Montparnasse-Bienvenüe**

D'Chez Eux (€€)

Bistro specialising in *cassoulet* (haricot-bean stew with Toulouse sausages). Terrace.

✉ **2 avenue Lowendal, 75007 Paris** ☎ **01 47 05 52 55** 🕐 **Lunch, dinner; closed Sun and first 3 weeks of Aug** Ⓜ **Ecole Militaire**

Côté Seine (€–€€)

Along the embankment between Notre-Dame and the pont Neuf. Good value for money; book ahead.

✉ **45 quai des Grands-Augustins, 75006 Paris** ☎ **01 43 54 49 73** 🕐 **Dinner** Ⓜ **Saint-Michel**

La Coupole (€€)

Famous brasserie from the 1920s with art deco setting; excellent seafood. Reasonable late-night menu (after 11PM).

✉ **102 boulevard du Montparnasse, 75014 Paris** ☎ **01 43 20 14 20** 🕐 **Daily 8:30AM–1PM** Ⓜ **Vavin**

La Criée (€)

For lovers of seafood at affordable prices!

✉ **15 rue Lagrange, 75005 Paris** ☎ **01 43 54 23 57** 🕐 **Lunch, dinner** Ⓜ **Maubert–Mutualité**

La Dinée (€€)

Imaginative cuisine with an emphasis on fish; young chef already hailed by gourmets.

✉ **85 rue Leblanc, 75015 Paris** ☎ **01 45 54 20 49** 🕐 **Lunch, dinner; closed Sat, Sun and 2 weeks in Aug** Ⓜ **Javel**

Le Divellec (€€€)

One of the top seafood restaurants in Paris complete with nautical décor, and very good service.

✉ **107 rue de l'Université, 75007 Paris** ☎ **01 45 51 91 96** 🕐 **Lunch, dinner; closed Sat, Sun, Christmas** Ⓜ **Invalides**

Le Dôme (€€–€€€)

Brasserie specialising in all types of seafood. Especially good is the *bouillabaisse* from Provence.

✉ **108 boulevard du Montparnasse, 75014 Paris** ☎ **01 43 35 25 81** 🕐 **Lunch, dinner** Ⓜ **Vavin**

L'Epi Dupin (€)

Sought-after, reasonably priced restaurant with regular change of menu; book well in advance. Best ingredients from Rungis market. Terrace.

✉ **11 rue Dupin, 75006 Paris** ☎ **01 42 22 64 56** 🕐 **Lunch, dinner; closed Sat, Sun, Mon lunch and 3 weeks in Aug** Ⓜ **Sèvres-Babylone**

La Frégate (€–€€)

Next to the Musée d'Orsay and facing the Louvre; good value traditional French cuisine.

✉ **35 quai Voltaire, 75007 Paris** ☎ **01 42 61 23 77** 🕐 **Lunch, dinner** Ⓜ **Rue de Bac**

Jacques Cagna (€€€)

High-class traditional French cuisine in 17th-century residence with wood panelling and beams; Dutch paintings to match.

✉ **14 rue des Grands-Augustins, 75006 Paris** ☎ **01 43 26 49 39** 🕐 **Lunch, dinner; closed Sat, Mon lunch, Sun, 1–21 Aug and Christmas** Ⓜ **Saint-Michel**

Mavrommatis (€–€€)
Refined traditional Greek cuisine; alfresco dining on the terrace in summer.
✉ **42 rue Daubenton, 75005 Paris** ☎ **01 43 31 17 17**
🕐 **Lunch, dinner; closed Mon**
🚇 **Censier-Daubenton**

Mon Vieil Ami (€€)
Recently opened restaurant; trendy rustic décor; delicious, reasonably priced dishes.
✉ **69 rue Saint-Louis-en-l'Île, 75004 Paris** ☎ **01 40 46 01 35**
🕐 **Lunch, dinner; closed Mon and Tue lunch** 🚇 **Pont-Marie**

La Parcheminerie (€–€€)
Charming bistro in picturesque pedestrian street of the Latin Quarter.
✉ **31 rue de la Parcheminerie, 75005 Paris** ☎ **01 46 33 65 12**
🕐 **Lunch, dinner; closed Sun and Mon** 🚇 **Saint-Michel; Cluny-la-Sorbonne**

Le Procope (€–€€)
An 18th-century literary café known to Voltaire and Benjamin Franklin, now a historic monument.
✉ **13 rue de l'Ancienne Comédie, 75006 Paris** ☎ **01 40 46 79 00** 🕐 **Lunch, dinner**
🚇 **Odéon**

La Régalade (€–€€)
Haute cuisine at relatively low prices in unassuming setting; book well in advance.
✉ **49 avenue Jean Moulin, 75014 Paris** ☎ **01 45 45 68 58**
🕐 **Lunch, dinner; closed Sat Sun and Mon lunch** 🚇 **Alesia**

Le Reminet (€–€€)
Refined bistro-style fare; terrace in summer. Extraordinarily good desserts. Friendly service.
✉ **3 rue des Grands-Degrés, 75005 Paris** ☎ **01 44 07 04 24**

🕐 **Lunch, dinner, closed Mon, Tue, 1–21 Jan and 15–31 Aug**
🚇 **St-Michel**

Susan's Place (€)
Convivial Tex Mex restaurant also serving vegetarian dishes.
✉ **51 rue des Écoles, 75005 Paris** ☎ **01 43 54 23 22** 🕐 **Lunch, dinner; closed Sun lunch, Mon** 🚇 **Maubert-Mutualité**

Thoumieux (€–€€)
High-class brasserie specialising in home-made duck *cassoulet*.
✉ **79 rue Saint-Dominique, 75007 Paris** ☎ **01 47 05 49 75**
🕐 **Lunch, dinner**
🚇 **Invalides**

La Tour d'Argent (€€€)
Haute cuisine served in exceptional surroundings with remarkable view of Notre-Dame and the river; speciality: *canard* (duck) *Tour d'Argent*.
✉ **15–17 quai de la Tournelle, 75005 Paris** ☎ **01 43 54 23 31**
🕐 **Lunch, dinner; closed Mon, Tue lunch** 🚇 **Pont-Marie**

La Truffière (€€)
Very refined cuisine served in pleasant surroundings. The menu makes good use of truffles, as the name suggests.
✉ **4 rue Blainville, 75005 Paris** ☎ **01 46 33 29 82** 🕐 **Lunch, dinner; closed Mon, 1–20 Aug**
🚇 **Place Monge**

Ze Kitchen Galerie (€€)
Trendy restaurant popular with the local crowd; innovative cuisine served in original surroundings.
✉ **4 rue des Grands-Augustins, 75006 Paris,** ☎ **01 44 32 00 32**
🕐 **Lunch, dinner; closed Sat lunch and Sun** 🚇 **Saint-Michel**

Where to Eat
Restaurants usually serve meals from midday to 2PM and from 7.30 to 10.30PM. *Brasseries* (the word means breweries) are restaurants where one can often eat at any time of the day and that often have *choucroute* on their menu, served with a glass of draught beer. Bistros are usually more modest (although some of them are very fashionable) and convivial, boasting quick, friendly service.

Ile de France

Prices
The same price rating as for Paris has been applied to restaurants in nearby towns; however, you can expect to get much better value for money outside the capital; it is also important to remember that service finishes earlier in the evening than in Paris, usually around 9:30.

Chantilly
🚉 Gare du Nord to Chantilly-Gouvieux

Château de la Tour (€€)
Refined cuisine and wood-panelled décor; terrace in summer.
✉ Chemin de la Chaussée, 60270 Gouvieux (1km from Chantilly) ☎ 03 44 62 38 38
🍴 Lunch, dinner

Condé Ste Libiaire (3km from Disneyland)
🚉 RER A Marne-la-Vallée/Chessy

La Vallée de la Marne (€–€€)
Peaceful setting; dining-room overlooks the garden on the banks of the River Marne. Fresh local produce.
✉ 2 quai de la Marne, 77450 Condé-Ste Libiaire ☎ 01 60 04 31 01 🍴 Lunch, dinner; closed Mon dinner, Tue

Fontainebleau
🚉 Gare de Lyon to Fontainebleau-Avon then 🚌 A or B

L'Atrium (€–€€)
Pizzeria in the town centre; with attractive year-round terrace dining.
✉ 20 rue France, 77300 Fontainebleau ☎ 01 64 22 18 36
🍴 Lunch, dinner

Le Caveau des Ducs (€€)
Elegant restaurant in vaulted cellars; terrace in summer.
✉ 24 rue Ferrare, 77300 Fontainebleau ☎ 01 64 22 05 05
🍴 Lunch, dinner

Le Montijo (€€)
Brasserie in luxury hotel facing the Château; terrace in summer.
✉ Grand Hôtel de l'Aigle Noir, 27 place Napoléon Bonaparte, 77300 Fontainebleau ☎ 01 60 74 60 00 🍴 Lunch, dinner

Drive In and Around the Forêt de Fontainebleau

Barbizon
L'Angélus (€€)
Convivial gastronomic restaurant with a terrace in summer.
✉ 31 rue Grande, 77630 Barbizon ☎ 01 60 66 44 30
🍴 Lunch, dinner; closed Tue

Hostellerie du Bas-Préau (€€–€€€)
Haute cuisine meals served in the garden. Queen Elizabeth II and Emperor Hiro Hito have both stayed here.
✉ 22 rue Grande, 77630 Barbizon ☎ 01 60 66 40 05
🍴 Lunch, dinner

Bourron-Marlotte (9km south of Fontainebleau)
Les Prémices (€€)
Within the Fontainebleau forest; dishes are served on the terrace in summer.
✉ 12 bis rue Blaise de Montesquiou. 77780 Bourron-Marlotte ☎ 01 64 78 33 00
🍴 Lunch, dinner; closed Sun dinner, Mon and first two weeks in August

Ruiel-Malmaison
🚉 RER Rueil-Malmaison

Le Fruit Défendu (€€)
Picturesque inn along the Seine; traditional French cuisine.
✉ 80 boulevard Belle-rive, 92500 Rueil-Malmaison
☎ 01 47 49 60 60 🍴 Lunch, dinner; closed Sun dinner, Mon

Saint-Cloud
🚇 Gare Saint-Lazare to Saint-Cloud

Quai Ouest (€€)
This 'Floating warehouse' serving appetising fish and poultry dishes is the place to go when the sun is out.
✉ 1200 quai Marcel Dassault, 92210 Saint-Cloud ☎ 01 46 02 35 54 🕐 Lunch, dinner

Saint-Denis
🚇 Métro Saint-Denis-Basilique

Campanile Saint-Denis Basilique (€)
One of a chain of inn-style modern hotels serving reliably good cuisine.
✉ 14 rue Jean-Jaurès, 93200 Saint-Denis ☎ 01 48 20 74 31 🕐 Lunch, dinner

Saint-Germain-en-Laye
🚇 RER Saint-Germain-en-Laye

Cazaudehore-La Forestière (€€€)
Sophisticated garden setting for refined summer meals; the menu even includes frogs' legs!
✉ 1 avenue du Président Kennedy, 78100 Saint-Germain-en-Laye ☎ 01 30 61 64 64 🕐 Lunch, dinner; closed Mon except hols

Ermitage des Loges (€€)
Reasonably priced, cuisine with an emphasis on fish and seafood. Summer eating is in the garden.
✉ 11 avenue des Loges, 78100 Saint-Germain-en-Laye ☎ 01 39 21 50 90 🕐 Lunch, dinner

Feuillantine (€)
You will find tasty cuisine at moderate prices in this elegant commuterland setting close to the impressive château.
✉ 10 rue Louviers, 78100 Saint-Germain-en-Laye ☎ 01 34 51 04 24 🕐 Lunch, dinner

10km from Vaux-Le-Vicomte
🚇 Gare de Lyon to Melun

La Mare au Diable (€€)
Lovely old house with beams (see panel); terrace for summer meals.
✉ RN6, 77550 Melun-Sénart ☎ 01 64 10 20 90 🕐 Lunch, dinner; closed Sun dinner, Mon

Versailles
🚇 Gare Saint-Lazare to Versailles Rive-Droite; RER C to Versailles Rive Gauche

Le Boeuf à la Mode (€)
Old-fashioned brasserie with sunny terrace serving excellent duck and vegetable spaghettis.
✉ 4 rue au Pain, 78000 Versailles ☎ 01 39 50 31 99 🕐 Lunch, dinner

La Cuisine Bourgeoise (€€)
Tasty refined cuisine served in cosy surroundings; perfect place to stop on a day out to Versailles.
✉ 10 boulevard du Roi, 78000 Versailles ☎ 01 39 53 11 38 🕐 Lunch, dinner; closed Sat lunch, Sun, Mon and 3 weeks in Aug

Le Potager du Roy (€–€€)
Extremely good-value bistro. Traditional dishes served in elegant surroundings.
✉ 1 rue du Maréchal-Joffre, 78000 Versailles ☎ 01 39 50 35 34 🕐 Lunch, dinner; closed Sun dinner and Mon

Drive through the Vallée De Chevreuse

Rambouillet
Le Cheval Rouge (€–€€)
Restaurant in the heart of the old town; traditional cuisine served in convivial setting; pleasant winter garden.
✉ 78 rue du Général-de-Gaulle, 78120 Rambouillet, ☎ 01 30 88 80 61 🕐 Lunch, dinner; closed Tue evening and Wed

La Mare au Diable
Memories of George Sand linger on in this 15th-century manor house, named after one of her most famous 'rural' novels; it was here that the young romantic Aurore Dupin met her future husband and later decided on her pen-name.

Paris

Prices

Prices indicated below are per room:

€ = budget (under €100)
€€ = moderate (€100–€200)
€€€ = expensive to luxury (over €200)

Note that luxury hotels such as the Ritz or the Crillon can charge over 700 euros for a double room. Payment can be made by credit cards in most hotels except in some budget hotels.

Hôtel de l'Abbaye (€€€)

A roaring log fire and a delightful inner garden ensure comfort whatever the season.

www.hotel-abbaye.com
✉ 10 rue Cassette, 75006 Paris
☎ 01 45 44 38 11 🕐 All year
Ⓜ Saint-Sulpice

Hôtel d'Angleterre Saint-Germain-des-Prés (€€–€€€)

The largest rooms of this quiet luxury hotel overlook the secluded garden.

✉ 44 rue Jacob, 75006 Paris
☎ 01 42 60 34 72 🕐 All year
Ⓜ St-Germain-des-Prés

Hôtel Caron de Beaumarchais (€€)

Recently restored 18th-century town house in the Marais; refined period decoration and air conditioning in all rooms.

www.carondebeaumarchais.com ✉ 12 rue Vieille-du-Temple, 75004 Paris ☎ 01 42 72 34 12 🕐 All year Ⓜ Hôtel de Ville

Hôtel Esmeralda (€)

Some rooms in this old-fashioned yet cosy hotel offer delightful views of Notre-Dame. Beware no lift!

✉ 4 rue Saint-Julien-le-Pauvre, 75005 Paris ☎ 01 43 54 19 20 🕐 All year Ⓜ Saint-Michel

Hôtel Franklin-Roosevelt (€€€)

Bright comfortable bedrooms with striking murals and functional bathrooms; warm welcome.

www.groupfrontenac.com/intro FRF.Rtm ✉ 18 rue Clément Marot, 75008 Paris ☎ 01 53 57 49 50 🕐 All year
Ⓜ Franklin-D Roosevelt

Hôtel Galileo (€€)

Modern refined hotel near the Champs-Elysées with air conditioning and well-appointed bedrooms, a few with verandas.

www.hotel-ile-saintlouis.com
✉ 54 rue Galilée, 75008 Paris
☎ 01 47 20 66 06 🕐 All year
Ⓜ George V

Hôtel du Jeu de Paume (€€€)

Exclusive hotel on the Ile Saint-Louis, housed in converted Jeu de Paume (inside tennis court), with striking galleries and mezzanines.

www.hoteljeudepaume.com
✉ 54 rue Saint-Louis-en-l'Ile, 75004 Paris ☎ 01 43 26 14 18
🕐 All year Ⓜ Pont-Marie

Hôtel du Lys (€)

Simple hotel at the heart of the Quartier Latin; no lift but modern bathrooms, warm welcome and reasonable prices; book well in advance.

✉ 23 rue Serpente, 75006 Paris
☎ 01 43 26 97 57 🕐 All year
Ⓜ Saint-Michel, Odéon

Hôtel Montalembert (€€€)

Luxury hotel, with discreet yet original decoration, sound-proofing and air conditioning; a quality hotel at top prices.

www.montalembert.com
✉ 3 rue de Montalembert, 75007 Paris ☎ 01 45 49 68 68
🕐 All year Ⓜ Rue du Bac

Hôtel de Nevers (€)

Simple but charming, in a former convent building; private roof terraces for top-floor rooms.

✉ 83 rue du Bac, 75007 Paris
☎ 01 45 44 61 30 🕐 All year
Ⓜ Rue du Bac

Hôtel du Panthéon (€€)
An elegant hotel conveniently situated in the university district, with well-appointed air-conditioned bedrooms.
www.hoteldupantheon.com
✉ 19 place du Panthéon, 75005 Paris ☎ 01 43 54 32 95 🕐 All year 🚇 Cardinal-Lemoine

Hôtel Place des Vosges (€)
Picturesque quiet hotel just off the place des Vosges.
✉ 12 rue de Birague, 75004 Paris ☎ 01 42 72 60 46 🕐 All year 🚇 Saint-Paul, Bastille

Hôtel Le Régent (€€)
Air conditioning and bright well-appointed bedrooms in this cleverly restored 18th-century house in St-Germain-des-Prés.
✉ 61 rue Dauphine, 75006 Paris ☎ 01 46 34 59 80 🕐 All year 🚇 Odéon

Hôtel Relais du Louvre (€€)
Warm colours, antique furniture and modern comfort, a stone's throw from the Louvre.
www.relaisdulouvre.com
✉ 19 rue des Prêtres Saint-Germain-l'Auxerrois, 75001 Paris ☎ 01 40 41 96 42 🕐 All year 🚇 Louvre-Rivoli

Résidence les Gobelins (€)
A haven of peace near the lively rue Mouffetard; warm welcome.
www.hotelgobelins.com
✉ 9 rue des Gobelins, 75013 Paris ☎ 01 47 07 26 90 🕐 All year 🚇 Les Gobelins

Hôtel Les Rives de Notre-Dame (€€€)
Elegant and comfortable, with sound-proofed bedrooms overlooking the quai Saint-Michel and the Ile de la Cité.
www.rivesdenotredame.com
✉ 15 quai Saint-Michel, 75005 Paris ☎ 01 43 54 81 16 🕐 All year 🚇 Saint-Michel

Hôtel Ritz Paris (€€€)
Sometimes called the palace of kings and the king of palaces, the Ritz shares with the Crillon the top of the list of Paris's luxury hotels. Overlooking the place Vendôme, it boasts a beautiful swimming pool and luxury fitness centre; prices are accordingly very high.
www.ritzparis.com
✉ 15 place Vendôme, 75001 Paris ☎ 01 43 16 30 70 🕐 All year 🚇 Opéra

Select Hôtel (€€)
Fully modernised hotel in the heart of the Latin Quarter, close to the Luxembourg gardens; cosy atmosphere; glass-roofed patio.
www.selecthotel.fr ✉ 1 place de la Sorbonne, 75005 Paris ☎ 01 46 34 14 80 🕐 All year 🚇 Cluny-la-Sorbonne; Odéon

Tim Hôtel Montmartre (€€)
In the old part of Montmartre, with lovely views; attention to detail makes it a comfortable if simple place to stay.
www.timhotel.com
✉ 11 rue Ravignan, 75018 Paris ☎ 01 42 55 74 79 🕐 All year 🚇 Abbesses

Hôtel Le Tourville (€€–€€€)
Refined decoration for this modern hotel in the elegant 7th *arrondissement*, close to Les Invalides.
www.tourville.com
✉ 16 avenue de Tourville, 75007 Paris ☎ 01 47 05 62 62 🕐 All year 🚇 Ecole Militaire

Historic Hotels
The Hôtel d'Angleterre was the seat of the British Embassy in the 18th century, at the time of American Independence; more recently, it was one of the temporary homes of Ernest Hemingway.
The Jeu de Paume, recently converted into a hotel, was built in the early 17th century as part of the development of the Ile Saint-Louis. It was the first one of its kind in Paris.
The exclusive Hôtel Ritz has had many famous guests, including the Duke of Windsor and Ernest Hemingway.

Ile de France

Country Hotels
The hotels listed in this section have been selected as much for their picturesque, even outstanding setting and surroundings as for their high level of comfort. The price range is the same as that of Paris hotels but these country hotels offer much better value for money.

Chantilly
🚉 Gare du Nord to Chantilly-Gouvieux

Château de Montvillargenne (€€–€€€)
Large mansion in vast own grounds; covered swimming pool, sauna, sports facilities.
www.chateaudemontvillargenne.com ✉ 1 avenue François Mathet, 60270 Gouvieux ☎ 03 44 62 37 37 🕐 All year

Château de la Tour (€€)
Late 19th-century mansion, with swimming pool, terrace and large park.
www.chateaudelatour.fr
✉ Chemin de la Chaussée, 60270 Gouvieux ☎ 03 44 62 38 38 🕐 All year

Le Relais d'Aumale (€€)
Former hunting-lodge of the Duc d'Aumale, at the heart of the Forêt de Chantilly.
http:/relais-aumale.fr
✉ 37 place des Fêtes, Montgresin 60560 Orry la Ville ☎ 03 44 54 61 31 🕐 All year

Disneyland
🚉 RER Marne-la-Vallée/Chessy

Cheyenne (€–€€)
Each of the hotels has its own authentic American theme; this one is self-explanatory.
☎ 01 60 45 62 00; UK booking centre: 08705 03 03 03 🕐 All year

Disneyland Hotel (€€€)
This Victorian-style hotel is the most sophisticated and expensive of the six hotels in the Disneyland complex and the closest to the theme park.
☎ 01 60 45 65 00; UK booking centre: 08705 03 03 03 🕐 All year

Magny-le-Hongre
Kyriad Disneyland Resort Paris (€)
Family-style modern hotel belonging to the Kyriad Hotel chain, very close to the Disneyland theme parks; shuttle service.
✉ 77700 Magny-le-Hongre ☎ 01 60 43 61 61 🕐 All year

Fontainebleau
🚉 Gare de Lyon to Fontainebleau-Avon

Grand Hôtel de l'Aigle Noir (€€€€)
Napoleon III-style decoration for this hotel facing the castle; fitness club, indoor swimming pool and very good restaurant.
www.hotelaiglenoir.fr
✉ 27 place Napoléon Bonaparte, 77300 Fontainebleau ☎ 01 60 74 60 00 🕐 All year

Drive in and Around the Forêt de Fontainebleau

Barbizon
Hôtel Les Charmettes (€)
Picturesque timber-framed Logis de France hotel.
www.lescharmettes.com ✉ 40 Grande-Rue, 77630 Barbizon ☎ 01 60 66 40 21 🕐 All year

Hostellerie de la Clé d'Or (€)
Former coaching-inn; rooms overlook the garden; terrace for summer meals.
✉ 73 Grande-Rue, 77630 Barbizon ☎ 01 60 66 40 96 🕐 All year

Hôtel Les Pléiades (€)
A former painter's house turned into a hotel in the

'painters' village! Splendid terrace for summer meals.

✉ 21 Grande-Rue, 77630 Barbizon ☎ 01 60 66 40 25

⏰ All year

Saint-Germain-en-Laye

🚇 RER Saint-Germain-en-Laye

Hôtel Cazaudehore-La Forestière (€€)

Relaxation is the keynote in this large hotel.

www.cazaudehore.fr

✉ 1 avenue du Président Kennedy, 78100 Saint-Germain-en-Laye ☎ Hotel: 01 39 10 38 38 ⏰ All year

Hôtel Ermitage des Loges (€€)

There's music on Wednesday and Thursday nights in the hotel bar; excellent restaurant.

www.ermitage-des-loges.fr

✉ 11 avenue des Loges, 78100 Saint-Germain-en-Laye ☎ 01 39 21 50 90 ⏰ All year

Pavillon Henri IV (€€–€€€)

Historic building near the famous Grande Terrasse; great views.

www.pavillonhenri4.fr

✉ 19–21 rue Thiers, 78100 Saint-Germain-en-Laye ☎ 01 39 10 15 15 ⏰ All year

Versailles

🚇 Gare Saint-Lazare to Versailles Rive Droite; RER C to Versailles Rive Gauche

Relais de Courlande (€)

Attractive converted 16th-century farmhouse; hydrotherapy facilities.

✉ 23 rue de la Division Leclerc, 78350 Les Loges-en-Josas ☎ 01 30 83 84 00

⏰ All year

Sofitel Château de Versailles (€€€)

Luxury Château hotel next to Château de Versailles.

www.sofitel.com ✉ 2bis avenue de Paris, 78000 Versailles ☎ 01 39 07 46 46

⏰ All year

Trianon Palace (€€€)

This luxury establishment, on the edge of the Parc de Versailles, boasts an exclusive fitness club, two tennis courts and golf and riding facilities. It is one of the top palace hotels in France.

www.trianonpalace.fr

✉ 1 boulevard de la Reine, 78000 Versailles ☎ 01 30 84 50 00 ⏰ All year

Drive through the Vallée De Chevreuse

Abbaye des Vaux de Cernay (€€–€€€)

A 12th-century Cistercian abbey, the setting for an unforgettable stay in the Vallée de Chevreuse; swimming pool, fitness club, tennis; musical evenings, *sons et lumières* show.

www.abbayedecernay.com

✉ 78720 Cernay-la-Ville (14km northeast of Rambouillet) ☎ 01 34 85 23 00 and 01 34 85 11 59 ⏰ All year

Auberge le Manet (€–€€)

A hotel in a former building of the 13th-century Abbaye de Port-Royal; set in its own grounds.

www.aubergedumanet.com

✉ 61 avenue du Manet, 78180 Montigny-le-Bretonneux (just north of the D91, ➤ 90, Vallée de Chevreuse drive) ☎ 01 30 64 89 00 ⏰ All year

Pavillon Henri IV

The lovely brick building of the Pavillon Henri IV, surmounted by a dome, is all that remains, together with another pavilion, of the Château Neuf erected at the beginning of the 17th century and demolished in the 18th century after being neglected for too long. King Louis XIV was actually born within its walls on 5 September 1638. The pavilion was turned into a hotel in 1836 and has subsequently attracted many famous guests.

Shopping in Paris

Opening Hours

Shops are usually open weekdays from 9–7. Some are closed on Mondays, others are open on Sundays. Smaller shops sometimes close for lunch. Food shops remain open later. Department stores close late on Thursdays (up to 10PM).

Duty-Free Shopping

Residents of non-EU countries are entitled to a VAT refund (about 12–13 per cent) if they spend over 175 euros in the same shop. Export receipts issued by shopkeepers must be presented on the day of departure to the Customs Officer, who may wish to see the goods. The refund will be credited within 30 days.
More information from: Centre de reuseignements des douanes ☎ 08 25 30 82 63 or Global Refund, www.globalrefund.com.

Department Stores

Bazar de l'Hôtel de Ville

Known as the BHV, this store is famous for its huge do-it-yourself department, which claims to be the place to find what you can't find anywhere else!
✉ 52–4 rue de Rivoli, 75001 Paris ☎ 01 42 74 90 00
Ⓜ Hôtel de Ville

Bon Marché Rive Gauche

The only department store on the Left Bank, and the first to open in Paris; famous for its Grande Epicerie, selling specialities from various countries and freshly prepared delicacies.
✉ 24 rue de Sèvres, 75007 Paris ☎ 01 44 39 80 00
Ⓜ Sèvres-Babylone

Galeries Lafayette

A few blocks away from Au Printemps, with designer ready-to-wear fashion and lingerie. Under a giant glass dome there is an enticing display of everything a home and its inhabitants need.
✉ 40 boulevard Haussmann, 75009 Paris ☎ 01 42 82 34 56
Ⓜ Chaussée d'Antin

Monoprix

Chain of department stores for the budget-conscious. There is a large branch at the back of Au Printemps.
✉ 52 avenue des Champs-Elysées, 75008 Paris ☎ 01 53 77 65 65 Ⓜ Franklin-D Roosevelt

Au Printemps

Three stores in one: Le Printemps de la Mode, including ready-to-wear designer fashion, Le Printemps de la Maison, including elegant tableware and hi-fi, record and stationery department in the basement, and Brummell, devoted to menswear.
✉ 64 boulevard Haussmann, 75009 Paris ☎ 01 42 82 50 00
Ⓜ Havre-Caumartin

Samaritaine

It lacks the stylishness of the boulevard Haussmann's stores but it offers a splendid view of Paris from the roof-top Toupary bistro.
✉ 19 rue de la Monnaie, 75001 Paris ☎ 01 40 41 20 20
Ⓜ Pont Neuf

Shopping Centres

Carrousel du Louvre

Elegant shopping centre located beneath the place du Carrousel and communicating with the Louvre; several boutiques connected with the arts, Virgin store and a number of bars serving food from different countries.
✉ 99 rue de Rivoli, 75001 Paris ☎ 01 43 16 47 47 Ⓜ Palais Royal

Drugstore Publicis

Unexpectedly situated at the top of the Champs-Elysées, a stone's throw from the Arc de Triomphe, this shopping mall has a restaurant and a selection of gift/souvenir shops.
✉ 133 avenue des Champs-Elysées, 75008 Paris ☎ 01 44 43 79 00 Ⓜ Charles de Gaulle-Etoile

Forum des Halles

Underground shopping centre on several floors including chain-store fashion boutiques and the new

Forum des Créateurs for young designers; also a huge FNAC store (▶ 107).
✉ 1–7 rue Pierre Lescot, 75001 Paris ⓠ Les Halles; RER Châtelet-Les Halles

Galeries Marchandes des Champs-Elysées
Several shopping malls link the Champs-Elysées and the parallel rue de Ponthieu between the Rond-Point des Champs-Elysées and the avenue George V; various boutiques including fashion and shoes.
✉ Avenue des Champs-Elysées, 75008 Paris
ⓠ George V, Franklin-D Roosevelt

Marché Saint-Germain
Fashion and gift shops including clothes, shoes, leather goods, accessories, perfume, jewellery and gifts.
✉ Rue Clément, 75006 Paris
ⓠ Mabillon

Trois Quartiers
Mainly traditional fashion boutiques in the exclusive Madeleine area.
✉ 23 boulevard de la Madeleine, 75001 Paris ☎ 01 42 97 80 12 ⓠ Madeleine

Fashion – Haute Couture

Chanel
✉ 31 rue Cambon, 75001 Paris
☎ 01 42 86 28 00 ⓠ Concorde

Christian Dior
✉ 30 avenue Montaigne, 75008 Paris ☎ 01 40 73 54 44 ⓠ Champs-Elysées Clémenceau

Emmanuel Ungaro
✉ 2 avenue Montaigne, 75008 Paris ☎ 01 53 57 00 00
ⓠ Alma-Marceau

Givenchy
✉ 3 avenue George V, 75008 Paris ☎ 01 44 31 50 00
ⓠ Alma-Marceau

Pierre Cardin
✉ 27 avenue de Marigny, 75008 Paris ☎ 01 42 66 68 98 and 01 42 66 64 74 ⓠ Champs-Elysées Clémenceau

Yves Saint-Laurent
✉ 7 avenue George V, 75008 Paris ☎ 01 56 62 64 00
ⓠ Alma-Marceau

Fashion – Boutiques and Accessories

Hermès
Silk scarves, leather goods.
✉ 24 rue du Faubourg Saint-Honoré, 75008 Paris ☎ 01 40 17 47 17 ⓠ Concorde

Jean-Paul Gaultier
Ready-to-wear fashion from this famous designer.
✉ 30 rue du Faubourg Saint-Antoine, 75012 Paris ☎ 01 44 68 84 84 ⓠ Bastille

Madelios
Male fashion from city suits to casuals and accessories.
✉ 23 boulevard de la Madeleine, Paris 75001 ☎ 01 53 45 00 00 ⓠ Madeleine

Nina Jacob
Trendy fashion and accessories.
✉ 23 rue des Francs-Bourgeois, 75004 Paris ☎ 01 42 77 41 20 ⓠ Saint-Paul

raoul et curly
Designer accessories, jewellery, perfumes, cosmetics, leather goods.
✉ 47 avenue de l'Opéra, 75002 Paris ☎ 01 47 42 50 10
ⓠ Opéra

Fashion
Most top fashion houses are located in the Concorde/Champs-Elysées area, in particular, avenue Montaigne, avenue Marigny and rue du Faubourg Saint-Honoré. Fashion boutiques selling ready-to-wear designer clothes are to be found in place des Victoires, in the Marais district (rue des Francs-Bourgeois), in the Palais-Royal area (rue Saint-Honoré), and in and around St-Germain-des-Prés (rue Saint-Sulpice, rue Bonaparte, rue de Rennes, rue de Sèvres and rue de Grenelle).

Shopping Arcades

A number of the covered shopping arcades built at the end of the 18th and the beginning of the 19th centuries still survive, retaining their old-world charm. Lined with boutiques and tea-rooms, they offer a moment's respite from the city's bustle. The most attractively decorated are the Galerie Vivienne, Galerie Colbert and Galerie Véro-Dodat, near the Palais-Royal. Others, such as the Passage Jouffroy along the Grands Boulevards, have a more exotic flavour.

Walter Steiger
Luxury shoes for men and women.
✉ 83 rue du Faubourg Saint-Honoré, 75008 Paris ☎ 01 42 66 65 08 Ⓜ Miromesnil

Yohji Yamamoto
Ready-to-wear clothes by the Japanese designer.
✉ 22 rue de Sèvres, 75007 Paris ☎ 01 45 44 29 32 Ⓜ St-Germain-des-Prés

High–Class Jewellers

Boucheron
✉ 26 place Vendôme, 75001 Paris ☎ 01 42 61 58 16 Ⓜ Opéra

Cartier
✉ 13 rue de la Paix, 75002 Paris ☎ 01 42 18 53 70 Ⓜ Opéra

Chaumet
✉ 12 place Vendôme, 75001 Paris ☎ 01 44 77 24 00 Ⓜ Opéra

Miscellaneous Gifts

Agatha
Fashion jewellery shop.
✉ 99 rue de Rivoli, 75001 Paris ☎ 01 42 96 03 09 Ⓜ Châtelet

Bernardaud
Porcelain, tableware, jewellery, original gifts.
✉ 11 rue Royale, 75008 Paris ☎ 01 47 42 82 86 Ⓜ Concorde, Madeleine

Lalique
Beautiful glass objects to suit every taste.
✉ 11 rue Royale, 75008 Paris ☎ 01 53 05 12 12 Ⓜ Concorde, Madeleine

Maison du Chocolat
Want to try the best chocolate in Paris?
✉ 225 rue du Faubourg Saint-Honoré, 75008 Paris ☎ 01 42 27 39 44 Ⓜ Ternes

Sic Amor
Fashion jewellery and accessories.
✉ 20 rue du Pont Louis-Philippe, 75004 Paris ☎ 01 42 76 02 37 Ⓜ Pont-Marie

Upla
Trendy gift shop.
✉ 5 rue St-Benoît, 75006 Paris ☎ 01 40 15 10 75 Ⓜ St-Germain des Prés

Art, Antiques and Handicrafts

Louvre des Antiquaires
This centre houses around 250 upmarket antique shops on three floors.
✉ 2 place du Palais-Royal, 75001 Paris ☎ 01 42 97 27 27 Ⓜ Palais-Royal

La Tuile à Loup
Handicrafts from various French regions.
✉ 35 rue Daubenton, 75005 Paris ☎ 01 47 07 28 90 Ⓜ Censier-Daubenton

Viaduc des Arts
Disused railway viaduct housing beneath its arches workshops and exhibitions displaying art and handicrafts.
✉ 9–129 avenue Daumesnil, 75012 Paris Ⓜ Bastille, Ledru-Rollin, Reuilly-Diderot

Village Saint-Paul
A group of small antique dealers established between rue Saint-Paul and rue Charlemagne.
✉ Le Marais, 75004 Paris Ⓜ Saint-Paul

Village Suisse

Very expensive antiques
displayed in the former
Swiss pavilions of the 1900
World Exhibition.

✉ **78 avenue de Suffren, 54 rue
de la Motte-Picquet, 75015 Paris**
Ⓜ **La Motte Picquet, Grenelle**

Books, CDs, Videotapes and Hi-Fi

The Abbey Bookshop

New and second-hand books
from Britain, Canada and the
USA.

✉ **29 rue de la Parcheminerie,
75005 Paris** ☎ **01 46 33 16 24**
Ⓜ **Saint-Michel**

FNAC

Books, hi-fi, videos, CDs,
cameras, computers, on
several floors.

✉ **28 avenue des Ternes, 75017
Paris (other branches in
Montparnasse, Les Halles and
Bastille)** ☎ **01 44 09 18 00**
Ⓜ **Ternes**

Gibert Joseph

Stationery, new and second-
hand books, CDs and videos.

✉ **26–30 boulevard Saint-
Michel, 75006 Paris** ☎ **01 44 41
88 88** Ⓜ **Odéon, Cluny-la-
Sorbonne, Luxembourg**

Shakespeare & Company

New and second-hand books
in English.

✉ **37 rue de la Bûcherie, 75005
Paris** ☎ **01 43 26 96 50**
Ⓜ **Maubert-Mutualité**

Village Voice

English-language bookshop.

✉ **6 rue Princesse, 75006 Paris**
☎ **01 46 33 36 47** Ⓜ **Mabillon**

W H Smith

Branch of the famous British
chain-store; reference and
children's books; guidebooks
in English and French.

✉ **248 rue de Rivoli, 75001
Paris** ☎ **01 44 77 88 99**
Ⓜ **Concorde**

Children's Shops

Agnès B Enfant

Smart children's clothes by
the fashionable designer.

✉ **2 rue du Jour, 75001 Paris**
☎ **01 40 39 96 88**
Ⓜ **Les Halles**

La Boutique de Floriane

Elegant children's clothes;
other branches in rue de
Sèvres, rue du Faubourg
Saint-Honoré, rue de
Grenelle, rue de Longchamp.

✉ **17 rue Tronchet, 75008 Paris**
☎ **01 42 65 25 95**
Ⓜ **Madeleine**

Chantelivre

Specialist bookshop dealing
with all the subjects that
interest children.

✉ **13 rue de Sèvres, 75006
Paris** ☎ **01 45 48 87 90**
Ⓜ **Sèvres-Babylone**

La Maison des Bonbons

Delicious sweets in all
shapes.

✉ **14 rue Mouton Duvernet
75014 Paris** ☎ **01 45 41 25 55**
Ⓜ **Mouton Duvernet**

Le Nain Bleu

The most famous toy shop in
Paris.

✉ **408 rue Saint-Honoré, 75008
Paris** ☎ **01 42 60 39 01**
Ⓜ **Concorde, Madeleine**

Food and Wines

Dubois et Fils

This temple to an amazing
range of cheese supplies
Paris's top restaurants!

'Carré Rive Gauche'

The 'square' formed along
the Left Bank by the quai
Voltaire, rue de
l'Université, rue du Bac
and rue des Saints-Pères,
which includes the rue de
Verneuil, rue de Lille and
rue de Beaune, is famous
for its high concentration
of antique dealers; every
year in May, the area
hosts the 'Cinq jours des
objets extraordinaires', an
exhibition of unusual
antique objects.

Art and Antiques

Antique dealers and art galleries are often concentrated in the same area: in the Marais, stroll along rue Vieille-du-Temple, rue Debelleyme and rue Saint-Gilles. On the Left Bank, rue Jacob and rue des Saints-Pères are particularly interesting. You can't browse in the exclusive shops in the avenue Matignon and rue du Faubourg Saint-Honoré, since you need an appointment to see the dealers! The Bastille area is definitely avant-garde and artists often exhibit in their own studios.

Open Late

Some shops at the heart of the city are open until midnight or later every night, including Virgin Mégastore and Drugstore Publicis in the Champs-Elysées and the chain store Prisunic in rue de la Boétie near by.

✉ 80 rue de Tocqueville, 75017 Paris ☎ 01 42 27 11 38 🚇 Malesherbes

Berthillon

Mouth-watering ice cream in a wide range of flavours.
✉ 31 rue Saint-Louis-en-l'Ile, 75004 Paris ☎ 01 43 54 31 61 🕐 Closed Mon and Tue 🚇 Pont-Marie

Les Caves Augé

For wine lovers. This is the oldest wine shop in Paris.
✉ 116 boulevard Haussmann, 75008 Paris ☎ 01 45 22 16 97 🕐 Closed one week in Aug 🚇 École-Militaire

Fauchon and Hédiard

Strictly for gourmets! Two delicatessen shops with high-quality French regional products.
✉ Fauchon at No 26, Hédiard at No 21 place de la Madeleine, 75008 Paris ☎ Fauchon: 01 47 42 91 10; Hédiard: 01 43 12 88 88 🚇 Madeleine

La Grande Épicerie de Paris

This huge grocery store is every gourmet's dreamland!
✉ 38 rue de Sèvres, 75007, Paris ☎ 01 44 39 81 00 🚇 Sèvres-Babylone

Lenôtre

Succulent cakes that melt in the mouth!
✉ 15 bd. de Courcelles, 75008 Paris ☎ 01 45 63 87 63 🚇 Villiers

Boulangerie Poîlane

The most famous bakery in Paris! Long queues form outside this shop for traditionally baked bread.
✉ 8 rue du Cherche-Midi, 75006 Paris ☎ 01 45 48 42 59 🚇 Sèvres-Babylone

La Maison du Miel

Delicately flavoured honey from various regions of France.
✉ 24 rue Vignon, 75008 Paris ☎ 01 47 42 26 70 🚇 Madeleine

Nicolas

Chain-stores selling a wide range of good French wines; at least one store per arrondissement.
✉ 189 rue Saint-Honoré, 75001 Paris ☎ 01 42 60 80 12 🚇 Palais-Royal

Markets

Carreau du Temple

Covered market specialising in leather and second-hand clothes.
✉ 75003 Paris 🕐 Tue–Fri 9–1:30, Sat 9–6, Sun 9–2 🚇 Temple, Arts et Métiers

Marché aux Fleurs

Picturesque daily market (8–7) that becomes a bird market on Sundays (8–7).
✉ Place Louis Lépine, Ile de la Cité, 75004 Paris 🚇 Cité

Marché aux Puces de Saint-Ouen

The largest flea market in Paris. Everything you can think of is for sale. Prices are often inflated, be prepared to bargain.
✉ Between Porte de Saint-Ouen and Porte de Clignancourt, 75017 Paris 🕐 Sat–Mon 8–6 🚇 Porte de Clignancourt

Marché aux Timbres

Stamp market for dealers and private collectors.
✉ Rond-Point des Champs-Elysées, 75008 Paris 🕐 Thu, Sat and Sun 9–7 🚇 Franklin-D Roosevelt

Shopping in the Ile de France

Meaux

Fromagerie de Meaux
Delicious Brie de Meaux and Coulommiers, two very tasty cheeses from Ile de France, made locally but famous nationwide.

✉ 4 rue du Général Leclerc, 77100 Meaux (11km north of Disneyland Paris) ☎ 01 64 34 22 82

Fontainebleau
🚉 Gare de Lyon to Fontainebleau-Avon, then 🚌 A or B

Boutique du Musée National de Fontainebleau
For history buffs fascinated by Napoleon I and European history at the beginning of the 19th century.

✉ Château de Fontainebleau, 77300 Fontainebleau ☎ 01 64 23 44 97

Drive in and Around the Forêt de Fontainebleau

Barbizon
Anabel's Galerie
Contemporary painting and sculpture.

✉ Le Bornage, 77630 Barbizon
☎ Fax: 01 60 69 23 96
🕐 Weekends only

Galerie d'Art Castiglione
One of more than 10 art galleries to be found in this popular artists' village.

✉ Grande rue, 77630 Barbizon
☎ 01 60 69 22 12

Soisy-sur-Ecole
Verrerie d'Art de Soisy
The Verrerie d'Art de Soisy has demonstrations of glass-blowing by the traditional rod method. Visitors will also have an opportunity to purchase ornamental glassware.

✉ Le Moulin de Noues, 91840 Soisy-sur-Ecole ☎ 01 64 98 00 03 🕐 Daily except Sun morning

Saint-Germain-en-Laye
🚉 RER Saint-Germain-en-Laye

Boutique du Musée des Antiquités Nationales
History books from prehistory to the early Middle Ages as well as reproductions of jewellery and various items from the museum's collections.

✉ Place du Château, 78100 Saint-Germain-en-Laye ☎ 01 39 10 13 22

Les Galeries de Saint-Germain
Close to the RER and the Château, 42 boutiques in les Galeries de Saint-Germain sell fashion, articles for the home and gifts; famous names include Chanel and Yves Saint-Laurent.

✉ 10 rue de la Salle, 78100 Saint-Germain-en-Laye ☎ 01 39 73 70 67 🕐 Closed Mon

Versailles
🚉 Gare Saint-Lazare to Versailles Rive Droite; RER C to Versailles Rive Gauche

Librairie-Boutique de l'Ancienne Comédie
There are 2,000 titles connected with the castle, its gardens and its history, many with information on 17th-and 18th-century architecture.

✉ Château de Versailles, passage des Princes, 78000 Versailles ☎ 01 30 83 76 90

Street Markets
It is a tradition in France to buy food, and in particular fresh vegetables and fruit, from a market stall and Paris is no exception. Each *arrondissement* has its covered market, but open-air ones are much more colourful and lively and their higgledy-piggledy displays are definitely more picturesque. To get the feel of these typical Parisian attractions, go to the rue Mouffetard (🚇 Monge), the rue de Buci (🚇 Odéon) and the rue Lepic (🚇 Abbesses). They are open daily except on Mondays.

Paris and the Ile de France

Eating Out
Some chain restaurants offer set junior menus, often for less than 7 euros. Batifol, Bistro Romain, L'entrecôte, Hippopotamus, Pomme de Pain, Pizza Hut (in Paris), Chantegrill, Côte à Côte, Courtepaille, Pizza del Arte (outside Paris). Any good restaurant will always suggest a choice of dishes for your children.

Interactive Museums
Most major museums organise themed visits and workshops for children from an early age, on Wed and Sat; in addition to the museums listed here, there are also the Carnavalet, Cognacq-Jay, Louvre, Mode et Costume, Orsay, and Palais de la Découverte museums in Paris, and the Château de Saint-Germain-en-Laye and Château de Versailles, outside Paris.

Paris

Museums
Cité des Sciences et de l'Industrie
Cité des Enfants: for the 3–5 and 5–12 age groups. Book as soon as you arrive. Techno cité: 11 years upwards.
Cinaxe: very effective simulator.
✉ **30 avenue Corentin-Cariou, 75019 Paris** ☎ **Information: 01 40 05 80 00** 🕐 **10–6; closed Mon** 🚇 **Porte de la Villette**

Musée de la Magie
Fascinating demonstrations of magic; workshops during school holidays.
✉ **11 rue Saint-Paul, 75004 Paris** ☎ **01 42 72 13 26** 🕐 **Wed, Sat and Sun 2–7** 🚇 **Saint-Paul**

Musée Grévin
Five hundred wax figures of the famous, from Henry VIII to Michael Jackson and Arnold Schwarzenegger!
✉ **10 boulevard Montmartre, 75009 Paris** ☎ **01 47 70 85 05** 🕐 **Mon–Fri 10–6:30; Sat–Sun 10–7** 🚇 **Rue Montmartre**

Musée de la Marine
Shows for 8–12 year-olds, with titles such as *Treasure Island*, on Wednesdays.
✉ **Palais de Chaillot, place du Trocadéro, 75016 Paris** ☎ **01 53 65 69 69** 🕐 **Wed 3PM** 🚇 **Trocadéro**

Musée National d'Histoire Naturelle
Spectacular procession of large and small animals in the Grande Galerie de l'Evolution.
✉ **57 rue Cuvier, 75005 Paris** ☎ **01 40 79 30 00** 🕐 **10–6; closed Tue** 🚇 **Jussieu, Gare d'Austerlitz**

Musée d'Orsay
A tour and a workshop to initiate 5–10 year-olds to painting and sculpture.
✉ **62 rue de Lille, 75007 Paris** ☎ **01 40 49 48 48** 🕐 **Jul and Aug Wed, Sat, Sun; phone for details** 🚇 **Solférino**

Outdoor Activities
Aquaboulevard
Aqualand with slides, heated pool, waves, beaches etc.
✉ **4–6 rue Louis Armand, 75015 Paris** ☎ **01 40 60 10 00** 🕐 **9AM–11PM (midnight on Fri and Sat)** 🚇 **Balard**

Jardin d'Acclimatation
Adventure park at the heart of the Bois de Boulogne.
✉ **Bois de Boulogne, 75016 Paris** ☎ **01 40 67 90 82** 🕐 **10–6; small train from Porte Maillot on Wed, Sat, Sun, hols 1:30–6** 🚇 **Sablons, Porte Maillot**

Jardin des Enfants aux Halles
An adventure ground for 7–11 year-olds.
✉ **Forum des Halles, 105 rue Rambuteau, 75001 Paris** ☎ **01 45 08 07 18** 🕐 **Oct–May 9–12 and 2–4 (Wed 10–4), closed Mon); Jul, Aug Tue, Thu, Fri 9–12 and 2–6; Wed, Sat 10–6, Sun 1–6** 🚇 **Les Halles**

Parc des Buttes-Chaumont
Cave, waterfall, lake, island and suspended bridge. Playgrounds for smaller children.
✉ **5 rue Botzaris, 75019 Paris** ☎ **01 42 38 02 63** 🕐 **7AM–9PM** 🚇 **Buttes-Chaumont**

Parc Zoologique de Paris
Located inside the Bois de Vincennes, this is much larger than the zoo of the Jardin des Plantes.

✉ 53 avenue de Saint-Maurice, 75012 Paris ☎ 01 44 75 20 10 (recorded information) 🕐 9–6 (6:30 Sun and bank hols) Ⓜ Porte Dorée

Shows

Circus shows

They are seasonal but there are always several available at any time in and around Paris; information is available in the weekly publications *Pariscope* and *l'Officiel des Spectacles*, both of which have a children's section.

Marionnettes du Champ-de-Mars

Indoor puppet show; two different shows every week.

✉ Champ-de-Mars (next to the Eiffel Tower), 75007 Paris ☎ 01 48 56 01 44 🕐 3.15 and 4.15; closed one week in Aug Ⓜ École-Militaire

Paris-story

Audio-visual show illustrating the history of Paris through its monuments.

✉ 11bis rue Scribe, 75009 Paris ☎ 01 42 66 62 06 🕐 9–7 on the hour Ⓜ Opéra

Ile de France

Outdoor Activities

Beach

There is a lovely beach at L'Isle-Adam on the banks of the Oise River (May–Sep).

✉ Plage de L'Isle-Adam, 95290 L'Isle-Adam (on the D922, ➤ 80) ☎ 01 34 69 41 99

Boat trips

Along the Oise, between l'Isle-Adam and Anvers.

✉ Tourisme Accueil Val d'Oise ☎ 01 30 29 51 00 🕐 May–Sep

Fontainebleau

Rowing on the Etang des Carpes in the park; little train through the town and park; cycling through the forest (cycle hire at the station); riding (☎ 01 60 72 22 40).

✉ Office du Tourisme, 4 rue Royale, 77300 Fontainebleau ☎ 01 60 74 99 99 Ⓜ Gare de Lyon to Fontainebleau-Avon

Mer de Sable

Lots to do for children of all ages, as well as shows inspired by the American Far West, magic shows, and spectacular horse-riding displays in the sand dunes.

✉ 60950 Ermenonville, A1 motorway, exit No 7 Survilliers-Ermenonville-Saint-Witz (close to Parc Astérix) ☎ 03 44 54 00 96 🕐 Apr–Sep 10:30–6:30 (variable, inquire beforehand) Ⓜ RER Roissy-Aéroport Charles de Gaulle, then shuttle to Ermenonville

Theme parks (see the individual entries for Disneyland Paris ➤ 81 and Parc Astérix ➤ 85)

Versailles

Cycle through the magnificent park (cycle hire at the end of the Grand Canal) or, for children, take a ride in the little train (departure from the Bassin de Neptune).

✉ 78000 Versailles ☎ Information: 01 30 83 78 00 🕐 7–sunset Ⓜ Gare Saint-Lazare-Versailles Rive Droite

Shows

Chantilly

Musée Vivant du Cheval: demonstration of dressage (daily) and horse show (1st Sun of every month).

✉ Grandes Ecuries, 60500 Chantilly ☎ 03 44 57 40 40 Ⓜ Gare du Nord to Chantilly-Gouvieux

Le Guignol du Parc de Saint-Cloud

Take a look at the puppet show in the park.

✉ Grille d'Orléans, route de Ville-d'Avray ☎ 01 48 21 75 37 🕐 Wed, Sun 3 and 4, Sat 4 Ⓜ Gare Saint-Lazare to Sèvres/Ville d'Avray

Monuments

The following are among children's favourites: Arc de Triomphe, Conciergerie (older children), Grande Arche de la Défense, Notre-Dame (the towers), Tour Eiffel, Château de Chantilly (stables), Château de Fontainebleau and Château de Versailles. For further information: www.iledenfrance.com

Sea Life Val d'Europe

Situated in the newly developed Val d'Europe complex, close to Disneyland Paris in Marne-la-Ville, this interactive marine-life centre includes some 30 aquariums displaying marine fauna and flora from around the world and offering an insight into endangered species schemes. Spectacular 360 degree tunnel!

✉ Centre Commercial International Val d'Europe, 14 cours du Danube, Serris, 77 Marne-la-Vallée. Take the A4 motorway towards Metz-Nancy, exit 14 ☎ 01 60 42 33 66 🕐 10–9

Entertainment in Paris

Nightlife News

Several brochures keep you up-to-date with events:

Weekly – *Pariscope* (including a *Time Out* selection in English) and *l'Officiel des Spectacles* issued Wednesday.

Monthly – *Paris Voice*, a free magazine available from English-language bookshops, highlights what's on in Paris: dance, theatre, music, art exhibitions…and comments on the latest trends; *www.parisvoice.com*. At any time on the internet – A weekly and monthly selection of events is available on the official website of the Office de Tourisme de paris, *www.paris-touristoffice.com*; in addition, *www.paris.org* has a very comprehensive 'Paris Calendar'.

Changing Fashion

Hip clubs come and go and DJs move around from one to the other, but some things remain constant: nothing really starts before midnight, some clubs have an entry fee that includes one drink, others charge more for their drinks. It pays to be smartly dressed to get past the door people; jeans and trainers are out.

Concert Venues

Cité de la Musique

This new temple of classical music regularly sets new trends with special commissions.

✉ **221 avenue Jean Jaurès, 75019 Paris** ☎ **01 44 84 45 45**
🚇 **Porte de Pantin**

Salle Pleyel

Traditional concert hall, named after one of France's most famous piano-makers, recently refurbished, and home to the Orchestre de Paris.

✉ **252 rue du Faubourg Saint-Honoré, 75008 Paris** ☎ **01 45 61 53 00** 🚇 **Ternes, Charles de Gaulle-Etoile**

Théâtre des Champs-Elysées

Paris's most prestigious classical concert venue with top international orchestras.

✉ **15 avenue Montaigne, 75008 Paris** ☎ **01 49 52 50 50**
🚇 **Alma-Marceau**

Théâtre du Châtelet

Classical concerts, opera performances, ballets and variety shows alternate in this 19th-century theatre that has welcomed great names such as Mahler and Diaghilev.

✉ **1 place du Châtelet, 75001 Paris** ☎ **01 40 28 28 40**
🚇 **Châtelet**

Zénith

This huge hall is the mecca of rock concerts, a privilege it shares with the Palais Omnisports de Paris Bercy (▶ 113).

✉ **211 avenue Jean Jaurès, 75019 Paris** ☎ **01 42 08 60 00**
🚇 **Porte de Pantin**

Cabaret and Music-Hall

Crazy Horse Saloon

One of the best shows in Paris with beautiful girls and striking colours and lights.

✉ **12 avenue George V, 75008 Paris** ☎ **01 47 23 32 32**
🚇 **Alma-Marceau**

Le Lido

The show put on by the famous Bluebell girls is still very effective. It is possible to have dinner on a *bateau-mouche* followed by a show at the Lido.

✉ **116 bis avenue des Champs-Elysées, 75008 Paris** ☎ **01 40 76 56 10** 🚇 **George V**

Moulin-Rouge

Undoubtedly the most famous of them all! The show still includes impressive displays of French can-can.

✉ **82 boulevard de Clichy, 75018 Paris** ☎ **01 53 09 82 82**
🚇 **Blanche**

Olympia

The most popular music-hall in France has been completely refurbished.
www.olympiahall.com
✉ **28 boulevard des Capucines, 75009 Paris**
☎ **08 92 68 33 68** 🚇 **Opéra**

Jazz Clubs

Bilboquet

Select establishment at the heart of St-Germain-des-Prés for serious jazz fans.

✉ **13 rue Saint-Benoît, 75006 Paris** ☎ **01 45 48 81 84**
🚇 **St-Germain-des-Prés**

Caveau de la Huchette

Jazz and rock mania let loose in medieval cellars!

✉ **5 rue de la Huchette, 75005 Paris** ☎ **01 43 26 65 05**
Ⓜ **Saint-Michel**

Nightclubs and Bars

Les Bains Douches
Hip rendezvous of models and VIPs, with different styles of music.
✉ **7 rue du Bourg-l'Abbé, 75003 Paris** ☎ **01 48 87 01 80**
Ⓜ **Etienne Marcel**

La Chapelle des Lombards
Salsa and Afro music; live shows mid-week.
✉ **19 rue de Lappe, 75011 Paris** ☎ **01 43 57 24 24** Ⓜ **Bastille**

La Casbah
Acid jazz and house alternate on different days with dance, disco music. Exotic décor.
✉ **18–20 rue de la Forge-Royale, 75011 Paris** ☎ **01 43 71 04 39** Ⓜ **Faidherbe-Chaligny**

Le Cithéa
Live music, disco, jazz, funk.
✉ **114 rue Oberkampf, 75011 Paris** ☎ **01 40 21 70 95**

Le Mambo Club
Exotic décor, Afro music, salsa...
✉ **20 rue Cujas, 75005 Paris** ☎ **01 43 54 89 21**
Ⓜ **Cluny-la-Sorbonne**

Zed Club
Rock, jazz, swing, salsa and 60s–90s pop.
✉ **20 rue des Anglais, 75005 Paris** ☎ **01 43 54 93 78**
Ⓜ **Saint-Michel; Maubert-Mutalité**

Rue Oberkampf
Music bars line this street, which teems with young Parisians in summer.
Ⓜ **Parmentier**

Sport

Piscine des Halles
Situated on Level 3 of Les Halles complex, this sports centre has a 50m-long underground swimming pool.
✉ **10 place de la Rotonde, 75001 Paris** ☎ **01 42 36 98 44**
Ⓜ **Les Halles**

Piscine Pontoise Quartier Latin
Fitness club with swimming pool, squash court, sauna.
✉ **19 rue de Pontoise, 75005 Paris** ☎ **01 55 42 77 88**
Ⓜ **Maubert-Mutualité**

Hippodrome d'Auteuil
Steeplechasing; Grand Steeplechase de Paris, mid-June.
✉ **Bois de Boulogne, 75016 Paris** ☎ **01 40 71 47 47**
Ⓜ **Porte d'Auteuil**

Hippodrome de Longchamp
Flat-racing; Grand Prix de Paris in late June, Prix de l'Arc de Triomphe in October.
✉ **Bois de Boulogne, 75016 Paris** ☎ **01 44 30 75 00**
Ⓜ **Porte Maillot and** 🚌 **244**

Hippodrome de Vincennes
Trotting races; Prix d'Amérique in late January.
✉ **2 route de la Ferme, 75012 Paris** ☎ **01 49 77 17 17**
Ⓜ **Château de Vincennes**

Palais Omnisports de Paris Bercy (POPB)
Around 150 international sporting events every year.
✉ **8 boulevard de Bercy, 75012 Paris** ☎ **01 40 02 60 60**
Ⓜ **Bercy**

Parc des Princes
The famous venue for national and international football and rugby matches.
✉ **24 rue du Commandant-Guilbaud, 75016 Paris** ☎ **08 25 07 50 78** Ⓜ **Porte de Saint-Cloud**

Roland Garros
Venue every year in late May and early June for the tennis tournament.
✉ **2 avenue Gordon Bennett, 75016 Paris** ☎ **01 47 43 48 00**
Ⓜ **Porte d'Auteuil**

Free Concerts
The municipality of Paris organises free concerts in the city's parks and gardens between May and September (programmes from the Office de Tourisme de Paris). Organ concerts on the 3rd Sunday of every month in selected venues (☎ 01 42 76 67 00). Some church concerts are free, for instance in the Madeleine and the American Church on Sunday and in Saint-Merri on Saturday and Sunday. Concerts broadcast from La Maison de Radio-France are open to the public and the entrance is free (information and reservations ☎ 01 42 30 22 22).

Cinemas and Theatres
There are some 350 cinema screens in Paris. Most large cinemas show several films at once. On Friday and Saturday nights, there are long queues outside cinemas in the Champs-Elysées and the Grands Boulevards. Paris is also well stocked with theatres from the grand Comédie Française (☎ 01 44 58 15 15), where French classics are performed, to the tiny local theatre where contemporary plays either hit the limelight or flop into oblivion.

Entertainment in the Ile de France

Tourist Offices
For information about the Ile de France, contact the following:

Espace du Tourisme d'Ile-de-France
✉ Carrousel du Louvre, 99 rue de Rivoli, 75001 Paris ☎ 08 26 16 66 66 within France and 01 44 50 19 98 from abroad

Espace du Tourisme d'Ile-de-France et de Seine et Marne
✉ Festival Disney, 77705 Marne-la-Vallée cedex 4 ☎ As for Espace du Touriseme above and www.pidf.com

Comité Départemental du Tourisme des Yvelines
✉ 2 place André Mignot, 78012 Versailles cedex ☎ 01 39 07 71 22, www.cg78.fr

Office National des Forêts, Direction Régionale Ile-de-France
✉ Boulevard de Constance, 77300 Fontainebleau ☎ 01 60 74 92 40

La Haute Vallée de Chevreuse
The Parc Naturel Regional de la Haute Vallée de Chevreuse was created in 1984 over an area of 25,000 ha, including 12,000 ha of woodland. It is criss-crossed by footpaths offering many opportunities for walks of 1½ to 3 hours. Information and itineraries are available from the Maison du Parc in Chevreuse.

Outdoor Activities

Boat trips
Croisières sur l'Oise
River cruise through the beautiful countryside lying between L'Isle-Adam and Auvers-sur-Oise.
☎ 01 30 29 51 00 🕐 Sun and holidays in summer

Golf
Disneyland Paris (27 holes)
Conveniently located near to the theme park and the Disneyland hotels.
✉ Allée de la Mare Houleuse, 77400 Magny le Hongre
☎ 01 60 45 68 90 🚆 RER to Marne-la-Vallée/Chessy

Fontainebleau (18 holes)
✉ Route d'Orléans, 77300 Fontainebleau ☎ 01 64 22 22 95 🚆 Gare de Lyon to Fontainebleau-Avon

Saint-Germain-en-Laye (27 holes)
Built in the Forêt de Saint-Germain by the Englishman Harry Colt.
✉ Route de Poissy, 78100 Saint-Germain-en-Laye
☎ 01 39 10 30 30 🚆 RER to Saint-Germain-en-Laye

Versailles: Golf de la Boulie (two 18-hole courses and one 9-hole course)
✉ Route du Pont Colbert, 78000 Versailles ☎ 01 39 50 59 41
🚆 Gare Saint-Lazare to Versailles Rive Droite

Hiking
Comité Régional de Randonnée Pédestre en Ile-de-France
Information on hiking in the seven *départements* of the Ile de France.
✉ 40 rue de Paradis, 75010

Paris ☎ 01 48 01 81 51
🚇 Plaisance, Pernéty

Horse-Racing
Hippodrome de Chantilly
Prix du Jockey-Club and Prix de Diane-Hermès in June.
✉ Route de l'Aigle, 60631 Chantilly ☎ 03 44 62 44 00
🚆 Gare du Nord to Chantilly-Gouvieux

Horse-Riding
Centre Equestre des Basses Masures
✉ Poigny-la-Forêt, 78125
☎ 01 34 84 70 29

Haras du Croc Marin
✉ Chemin rural des Trembleaux, 77690 Montigny-sur-Loing
☎ 01 64 45 84 01

Leisure Parks
Saint-Quentin-en-Yvelines
Rambling nature trails, a wide range of sporting activities, children's playground, cycle hire etc.
✉ D912, 78190 Trappes (7km west of Versailles) ☎ 01 30 62 20 12 🚆 RER C to Saint-Quentin-en-Yvelines (10-minute walk)

Torcy
Cycling, pony-trekking, windsurfing, canoeing etc.
✉ Route de Lagny, 77200 Torcy (9km west of Disneyland Paris) ☎ 01 64 80 58 75 🚆 RER to Torcy then 🚌 421

Mountain Bike Trails
Several itineraries through the Forêt de Fontainebleau.
Office du Tourisme ✉ 4 rue Royale, 77300 Fontainebleau
☎ 01 60 74 99 99 🚆 Gare de Lyon to Fontainebleau-Avon

Nature Park
Parc Naturel Régional de la Haute Vallée de Chevreuse
Themed nature trails: obtain

information from the Maison du Parc in Chevreuse.

✉ **La Maison du Parc, Château de la Madeleine, 78460 Chevreuse (▶ 90)** ☎ **01 30 52 09 09**

Concerts

Festival de Sceaux
International festival of chamber music from July to mid-September.

✉ **Orangerie du Domaine de Sceaux, 92330 Sceaux**
☎ **01 46 60 07 79**

Saison Musicale de Royaumont
Concerts in the lovely 12th-century abbey from June to September.

✉ **Abbaye de Royaumont, 95270 Asnières-sur-Oise (▶ 80)**
☎ **01 30 35 59 00**

Soirées Musicales au Château de Versailles
Concerts of baroque music on Thursdays and Saturdays, from November to June in the Opera house and the Royal Chapel. Information from the Centre de Musique Baroque de Versailles.

✉ **22 avenue de Paris, 78000 Versailles** ☎ **01 39 20 78 00**

Shows

Disneyland Paris
Buffalo Bill's Wild West Show
A fast moving dinner-show in the company of Buffalo Bill busy conquering the American Wild West.

☎ **Bookings: 01 60 45 71 00**

Disney Village
Just outside the theme park, restaurants, clubs, bars and shops open late into the evening. Also, there is a multiple-screen cinema and regular live concerts.

✉ **Disneyland Paris, 77777 Marne-la-Vallée** ☎ **01 60 30 60 30**

Meaux (11km north of Disneyland Paris)
Fe'erie Historique de Meaux
Son et Lumière show on a historical theme, lasting 1½ hours June–September. Information and bookings from Office de Tourisme de la Ville de Meaux.

✉ **2 rue St-Rémy, 77100 Meaux**
☎ **01 64 33 02 26**

Vaux-le-Vicomte
Visites aux Chandelles
Tours of the Château de Vaux-le-Vicomte by candlelight take place every Saturday night from May to mid-October.

✉ **Château de Vaux-le-Vicomte, 77950 Maincy**
☎ **01 64 14 41 90** 🚇 **Gare de Lyon to Melun then taxi**

Versailles
Grandes Eaux Musicales
There is a popular display of fountains with music held in the beautiful park of the Château de Versailles, every Sunday afternoon from May to October.

Grande Fête de Nuit
Son et Lumière show illustrating Louis XIV's life in the Château de Versailles and ending in a magnificent fire-works display; takes place seven times during the summer. Contact the Office de Tourisme for information.

✉ **Grandes Écuries du Roy, 78000 Versailles** ☎ **01 30 83 78 89** 🚇 **Gare Saint-Lazare to Versailles Rive Droite**

Fountains in the Parc de Versailles
Louis XIV wanted all the fountains in the park to work simultaneously. In order to achieve this, Le Nôtre worked for ten years with several engineers, dug 60km of channels and laid 11km of underground piping linking 15 small lakes and eight artificial ones!

What's On When

Check First!
The venues of the events listed here are liable to change from one year to the next and in the case of major festivals, there is often more than one venue. Dates also vary slightly from year to year. Information and programmes are available from:

Office de Tourisme de Paris
✉ 127 avenue des Champs-Elysées, 75008 Paris ☎ 08 36 68 31 12, www.paris-touristoffice.com ⊚ Charles de Gaulle-Etoile

Espace Régional du Tourisme Ile-de-France
✉ Carrousel du Louvre, 99 rue de Rivoli, 75001 Paris ☎ 08 03 81 80 00, www.paris-ile-de-france.com ⊚ Palais-Royal

Paris

June
Festival Chopin: An annual tribute to the Romantic composer at the Orangerie de Bagatelle in the heart of the Bois de Boulogne.
Fête de la Musique: On 21 June, Paris's squares, gardens and streets become alive with hundreds of musicians.
Festival de théâtre: Open-air theatre in English and in French, Jardin de Pré Catelan in the Bois de Boulogne.

June–July
Paris Jazz Festival: Open-air concerts in the Parc Floral de Paris, Bois de Vincennes.
14 July: Military parade down the Champs-Elysées, fireworks and popular ball to celebrate National Day.

July–August
Fête des Tuileries: Jardin des Tuileries becomes a fairground (begins end of June).
Paris, Quartier d'Eté: Open-air music, plays and dance.

September
Biennale Internationale des Antiquaires: Biennial International antiques display,(even years); last two weeks of September.
La Villette Jazz Festival: Jazz in the Grande Halle and the Parc de la Villette.

October
Foire Internationale d'Art Contemporain: Exhibition of contemporary art.
Mondial de l'Automobile: International motor-car show every two years (even years).

November–December
Salon Nautique International: International boat show.

Ile-de-France

April–May
Salon des Antiquaires de Rambouillet: Antique fair.

May–June
Festival de Saint-Denis: Symphonic concerts take place in Saint-Denis Basilica.
Festival d'Auvers-sur-Oise: Singing, piano and chamber music with famous artists.
Fête Médiévale: Medieval pageant, siege warfare demonstrations, tournaments in the historic city of Provins.
Le Mois Moière: Theatre, music and street entertainment in parts of the city of Versailles.

July–August
Fête des Loges de Saint-Germain-en-Laye: A fair held in Saint-Germain forest.

July–September
Festival de l'Orangerie de Sceaux: Chamber music festival in parc de Sceaux.

August
Fête de la Saint-Louis à Fontainebleau: An ancient royal tradition celebrated by fireworks at the Château.

September
Fête du Cheval Fontainebleau: International gathering of horse lovers.
Barbizon au temps des peintres... : Recalls 1848–70, when Forêt de Fontainebleau drew artists to Barbizon.

September–mid-October
Festival d'Ile-de-France: Concerts and shows in castles, abbeys and churches throughout the region.

Practical Matters

Above: *Les Halles – old and new*
Right: *Egyptian obelisk, place de la Concorde*

117

TIME DIFFERENCES

GMT
12 noon

France
1PM →

Germany
1PM →

USA (NY)
7AM ←

Netherlands
1PM →

Spain
1PM →

BEFORE YOU GO

WHAT YOU NEED

● Required ○ Suggested ▲ Not required	Some countries require a passport to remain valid for a minimum period (usually at least six months) beyond the date of entry – contact their consulate or embassy or your travel agent for details.	UK	Germany	USA	Netherlands	Spain
Passport/National Identity Card		●	●	●	●	●
Visa (Regulations can change – check before your journey)		▲	▲	▲	▲	▲
Onward or Return Ticket		▲	▲	▲	▲	▲
Health Inoculations		▲	▲	▲	▲	▲
Health Documentation (► 123, Health)		●	●	●	●	●
Travel Insurance		○	○	○	○	○
Driving Licence (national)		●	●	●	●	●
Car Insurance Certificate (if own car)		●	●	●	●	●
Car Registration Document (if own car)		●	●	●	●	●

WHEN TO GO

Paris

High season

Low season

7°C	7°C	10°C	16°C	17°C	23°C	25°C	26°C	21°C	16°C	12°C	8°C
JAN	FEB	MAR	APR	MAY	JUN	JUL	AUG	SEP	OCT	NOV	DEC

 Wet   Cloud   Sun   Sunshine & showers

TOURIST OFFICES

In the UK
French Tourist Office,
178 Piccadilly,
London W1J 9AL
☎ 09068 244123
Fax: (020) 7493 6594

In the USA
French Government
Tourist Office,
444 Madison Avenue,
16th floor,
New York NY10022
☎ 410 286 8310
Fax: 212/838 7855

French Government
Tourist Office,
9454 Wilshire Boulevard,
Suite 715,
Beverly Hills CA90212
☎ 310/271 6665
Fax: 310/276 2835

POLICE 17

FIRE 18

AMBULANCE 15

DOCTOR (24-hour call out) 01 47 07 77 77

WHEN YOU ARE THERE

ARRIVING

Paris has two main airports, Roissy-Charles-de-Gaulle (01 48 62 22 80), where most international flights arrive, and Orly (01 49 75 15 15). Eurostar trains, direct from London to Paris (☎ 0870 518 6186 in Britain, ☎ 08 92 35 35 39 in France), take 3 hours.

Roissy/Charles-de-Gaulle Airport

Kilometres to city centre	Journey times
23 kilometres	🚇 45 minutes
	🚂 50 minutes
	🚌 30–60 minutes

Orly Airport

Kilometres to city centre	Journey times
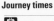 **14 kilometres**	🚇 40 minutes
	🚂 30 minutes
	🚌 20–40 minutes

MONEY

The euro is the official currency of France. Euro banknotes and coins were introduced in January 2002. Banknotes are in denominations of 5, 10, 20, 50, 100, 200 and 500 euros and coins are in denominations of 1, 2, 5, 10, 20 and 50 cents, and 1 and 2 euros. Euro traveller's cheques are widely accepted, as are major credit cards. Credit and debit cards can also be used for withdrawing euro notes from cashpoint machines. Cashpoints are widely accessible throughout the city. France's former currency, the French franc, went out of circulation in early 2002.

TIME

 France is on Central European Time (GMT+1). From late March, when clocks are put forward one hour, until late October, French summer time (GMT +2) operates.

CUSTOMS

→ **YES**

From another EU country for personal use (guidelines): up to 3,200 cigarettes, 400 cigarillos, 200 cigars, 3kg tobacco, 10 litres of spirits (over 22%), 20 litres of aperitifs, 90 litres of wine, 110 litres of beer.

From a non-EU country for personal use, the allowances are: 200 cigarettes OR 50 cigars OR 250g tobacco, 1 litre spirits (over 22%), 2 litres of wine, 2 litres of intermediary products (eg sherry) and sparkling wine, 50g perfume, 0.25 litres of eau de toilette. The value limit for goods is 175 euros.

Travellers under 17 years of age are not entitled to the tobacco and alcohol allowances.

 NO

Drugs, firearms, ammunition, offensive weapons, obscene material, unlicensed animals.

EMBASSIES

UK
☎ 01 44 51 31 00

Germany
☎ 01 53 83 45 00

USA
☎ 01 43 12 22 22

Netherlands
☎ 01 40 62 33 00

Spain
☎ 01 44 43 18 00

WHEN YOU ARE THERE

TOURIST OFFICES

Head Office
● Office de Tourisme de Paris (Paris Tourism Bureau), 25 rue des Pyramides, 75001 Paris
☎ 08 92 68 30 00 (omit the initial 0 when caling from outside France)
Fax: 01 49 52 53 00
www.paris-touristoffice.com

Branches
● Opéra-Grands Magasins
🕐 Mon–Sat 9AM–6.30PM

● Gare de Lyon
🕐 Mon–Sat 8AM–6PM

● Gare du Nord
🕐 Daily 8AM–6PM

● Montmartre (place du Tertre)
🕐 Daily 10AM–7PM

● Tour Eiffel (Eiffel Tower)
🕐 May–Sep: daily 11AM–6:40PM

Paris Île-de-France

● Carrousel du Louvre (lower level)
☎ 01 44 50 19 98/08 26 16 66 66
www.pidf.com
🕐 Daily 10AM–7PM

● Disneyland Resort Paris place des Passagers-du-Vent, Marne-la-Vallée, 77705
☎ 01 60 43 33 33
🚆 RER line A, Marne-la-Vallée–Parc Disneyland

NATIONAL HOLIDAYS

J	F	M	A	M	J	J	A	S	O	N	D
1		(1)	(1)	3(4)	(1)	1	1			2	1

1 Jan	New Year's Day
Mar/Apr	Easter Sunday and Monday
1 May	Labour Day
8 May	VE Day
May	Ascension Day
May/Jun	Whit Sunday and Monday
14 July	Bastille Day
15 Aug	Assumption Day
1 Nov	All Saints' Day
11 Nov	Remembrance Day
25 Dec	Christmas Day

Banks, businesses, museums and most shops (except boulangeries) are closed on these days.

OPENING HOURS

○ Shops   ● Museums/Monuments
● Offices   ● Churches
● Banks   ● Pharmacies

| 8AM | 9AM | 10AM | NOON | 2PM | 3PM | 4PM | 5PM | 6PM |

☐ Day   ☐ Midday
☐ Evening

In addition to the times shown above, some shops close between noon and 2PM and all day Sunday and Monday. Large department stores open from 9:30AM to 6:30PM and until 9 or 10PM one or two days a week. Food shops open 7AM to 1:30PM and 4:30 to 8PM; some open Sunday until noon. Some banks are open extended hours, including Saturday morning but most banks close weekends. Museum and monument opening times vary but national museums close Tuesday (except the Musée d'Orsay, Versailles and the Trianon Palace which close Monday), while most other city museums usually close Monday.

DRIVE ON THE RIGHT

TOILETS CHARGE

PUBLIC TRANSPORT

 Internal Flights Air France is the leading domestic airline – information (☎ 08 20 82 08 20). Daily departures from Orly and Roissy/Charles-de-Gaulle airports connect Paris with major French cities/towns in an average flight time of one hour.

 RER The RER (pronounced 'ehr-oo-ehr') is the fast suburban rail service, which also serves the city centre. There are five lines (*lignes*): A, B, C, D and E and it is connected with the métro and SNCF suburban network. Services run 5:30AM to midnight, with trains every 12 minutes.

 Métro Paris's underground with over 300 stations ensures you are never more than 500m from a métro stop. Lines are numbered 1 to 14 and are known by the names of the stations at each end. Follow the orange *correspondance* signs to change lines. The métro runs daily 5:30AM to 12:30AM.

 Buses Buses are a good way of seeing Paris (especially route 24), although traffic can be very heavy. Bus stops show the numbers of buses that stop there. Buses run 6:30AM to 8:30PM with a reduced service on Sunday and after 8:30PM. Bus tickets are the same as those for the métro.

 Boat The Batobus river shuttle (☎ 01 44 11 33 99) that plies the Seine from April to September provides an unusual view of Paris. It stops by the Eiffel Tower, Musée d'Orsay, the Louvre, Notre-Dame and the Hôtel de Ville; every 35 minutes, 10AM to 7PM (flat fare or all-day unlimited travel ticket).

CAR RENTAL

 Car-rental companies have desks at Roissy/ Charles-de-Gaulle and Orly airports, and in Paris itself. Car hire is expensive but airlines and tour operators offer fly-drive, and French Railways (SNCF) – train/car, packages that are cheaper than hiring locally.

TAXIS

 Taxis can be hailed if you see one with its roof light on. Taxis are metered with a surcharge for luggage, journeys after 10PM and before 6:30AM, and for going from and to stations and airports. Queues can be vast, particularly at railway stations.

DRIVING

 Speed limits on toll motorways (*autoroutes*) **130kph (110kph** when wet). Non-toll motorways and dual carriageways: **110kph (100kph** when wet). Paris ring road (*périphérique*): **80kph**.

 Speed limits on country roads: **90kph (80kph** when wet)

 Speed limits on urban roads: **50kph**

 Must be worn in front seats at all times and in rear seats where fitted.

 Random breath-testing. Never drive under the influence of alcohol.

 Leaded petrol is sold as *essence super* (98 octane). Unleaded is available in two grades: *essence sans plomb* (95 octane) and *essence super sans plomb* (98 octane). Diesel (*Gasoil* or *Gazole*) is also readily available. In Paris filling stations can be hard to spot, often consisting of little more than a few kerb-side pumps.

 If your car breaks down in Paris, contact the 24-hour repair service (☎ 01 45 31 16 20). On motorways (*autoroutes*) use the orange-coloured emergency phones (located every 2km) to contact the breakdown service.

PERSONAL SAFETY

Petty crime, particularly theft of wallets and handbags is fairly common in Paris. Be aware of innocent, scruffy-looking children, they may be working the streets in gangs, fleecing unwary tourists. Report any loss or theft to the *Police Municipale* (blue uniforms). To be safe:

● Watch your bag on the métro, in busy tourist areas like Beaubourg and the Champs-Elysées and in museum queues.
● Cars should be well-secured.
● Keep valuables in your hotel safe.

Police assistance:
☎ **17** from any call box

TELEPHONES

All telephone numbers in France comprise ten digits. Paris and Ile de France numbers all begin with 01. There are no area codes, simply dial the number. Most public phones use a phone-card (*télécarte*) sold in units of 50 or 120 from France Telecom shops, post offices, tobacconists and railway stations. Cafés have phones that take coins.

International Dialling Codes

From France to:

UK:	**00 44**
Germany:	**00 49**
USA:	**00 1**
Netherlands:	**00 31**
Spain:	**00 34**

POST

Post offices
Post offices are identified by a yellow or brown 'La Poste' or 'PTT' sign. Paris's main post office at 52 rue du Louvre is open 24 hours. ☎ 01 40 28 76 00. The branch at 71 avenue des Champs-Elysées opens Mon–Fri 9AM–7:30PM, Sat 10AM–7:30PM. Other branches: ● 8–7 (12 Sat); closed Sun

ELECTRICITY

The power supply in Paris is: 220 volts

Sockets accept two-round-pin (or increasingly three-round-pin) plugs, so an adaptor is needed for most non-Continental appliances and a voltage transformer for appliances operating on 100–120 volts.

TIPS/GRATUITIES

Yes ✓ No ✗		
Hotels (service included)	✓	(change)
Restaurants (service included)	✓	(change)
Cafés (service included)	✓	(change)
Taxis	✓	(1euro)
Tour guides	✓	(1 euro)
Porters	✓	(1 euro)
Usherettes	✓	(30c)
Hairdressers	✓	(1 euro)
Cloakroom attendants	✓	(15–30c)
Toilets	✓	(change)

PHOTOGRAPHY

What to photograph: Paris's monumental buildings and animated Parisians drinking in pavement cafés.

Where you need permission to photograph: certain museums will allow you to photograph inside. In churches with mural paintings and icons where flashlight is required permission must be sought first.

Where to buy film: shops and photo laboratories sell the most popular brands and types of film. Rapid film development is possible but quite expensive.

HEALTH

Insurance

Nationals of EU countries can obtain medical treatment at reduced cost in France with the relevant documentation (Form E111 for Britons), although private medical insurance is still advised and is essential for all other visitors.

Dental Services

As for general medical treatment (see above, **Insurance**), nationals of EU countries can obtain dental treatment at reduced cost. Around 70 per cent of standard dentists' fees are refunded. Still, private medical insurance is advised for all.

Sun Advice

July and August (when most Parisians leave the city) are the sunniest (and hottest) months. If 'doing the sights' cover up or apply a sunscreen and take on plenty of fluids. To escape the sun altogether spend the day visiting a museum.

Drugs

Pharmacies – recognised by their green cross sign – possess highly qualified staff able to offer medical advice, provide first-aid and prescribe a wide range of drugs, though some are available by prescription (*ordonnance*) only.

Safe Water

It is quite safe to drink tap water in Paris and all over France, but never drink from a tap marked *eau non potable* (not drinking water). Many prefer the taste of mineral water, which is fairly cheap and widely available in several brands.

CONCESSIONS

Students/Youths Holders of an International Student Identity Card (ISIC) are entitled to half-price admission to museums and sights and discounted air and ferry tickets, plus cheap meals in some student cafeterias. Those under 26, but not a student, with the International Youth Travel Card (or GO 25 Card) qualify for similar discounts as ISIC holders.

Senior Citizens Visitors over 60 can get discounts (up to 50 per cent) in museums, on public transport and in places of entertainment. Discounts apply to holders of the *Carte Senior*, which can be purchased from the *Abonnement* office of any main railway station. Without the card, show your passport and you may still get the discount.

CLOTHING SIZES

France	UK	Rest of Europe	USA		
46	36	46	36	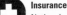	Suits
48	38	48	38		
50	40	50	40		
52	42	52	42		
54	44	54	44		
56	46	56	46		
41	7	41	8		Shoes
42	7.5	42	8.5		
43	8.5	43	9.5		
44	9.5	44	10.5		
45	10.5	45	11.5		
46	11	46	12		
37	14.5	37	14.5		Shirts
38	15	38	15		
39/40	15.5	39/40	15.5		
41	16	41	16		
42	16.5	42	16.5		
43	17	43	17		
36	8	34	6		Dresses
38	10	36	8		
40	12	38	10		
42	14	40	12		
44	16	42	14		
46	18	44	16		
38	4.5	38	6		Shoes
38	5	38	6.5		
39	5.5	39	7		
39	6	39	7.5		
40	6.5	40	8		
41	7	41	8.5		

WHEN DEPARTING

- Contact the airport or airline on the day prior to leaving to ensure flight details are unchanged.
- It is advisable to arrive at the airport two hours before the flight is due to take off.
- Check the duty-free limits of the country you are entering before departure.

LANGUAGE

You will usually hear well-enunciated French in Paris, spoken quite quickly and in a myriad of accents as many Parisians come from the provinces. English is spoken by those involved in the tourist trade and by many in the centre of Paris – less so in the outskirts. However, attempts to speak French will always be appreciated. Below is a list of a few words that may be helpful. The gender of words is indicated by (m) or (f) for masculine and feminine. More extensive coverage can be found in the AA's *Essential French Phrase Book* which lists over 2,000 phrases and 2,000 words.

hotel	*hôtel (m)*	rate	*tarif (m)*
room	*chambre (f)*	breakfast	*petit déjeuner (m)*
..single/double	*une personne /deux personnes (f)*	toilet	*toilette (f)*
...one/two nights	*une/deux nuits (f)*	bathroom	*salle de bain (f)*
...per person/per room	*par personne/par chambre*	shower	*douche (f)*
		balcony	*balcon (m)*
		key	*clef/clé (f)*
reservation	*réservation (f)*	room service	*service de chambre*
bank	*banque (f)*	English pound	*livre sterling (f)*
exchange office	*bureau de change (m)*	American dollar	*dollar (m)*
		banknote	*billet (m)*
post office	*poste (f)*	coin	*pièce (f)*
cashier	*caissier (m)*	credit card	*carte de crédit (f)*
foreign exchange	*change (m)*	traveller's cheque	*chèque de voyage (m)*
currency	*monnaie (f)*	giro cheque	*chèque postal (m)*
restaurant	*restaurant (m)*	starter	*hors d'oeuvres (m)*
café	*café (m)*	main course	*plat principal (m)*
table	*table (f)*	dish of the day	*plat du jour (m)*
menu	*carte (f)*	dessert	*dessert (m)*
set menu	*menu (m)*	drink	*boisson (f)*
wine list	*carte des vins (f)*	waiter	*garçon (m)*
lunch	*déjeuner (m)*	waitress	*serveuse (f)*
dinner	*dîner (m)*	the bill	*addition (f)*
aeroplane	*avion (m)*	...first/second class	*première/deuxième classe (f)*
airport	*aéroport (m)*		
train	*train (m)*	ticket office	*guichet (m)*
...station	*gare (f)*	timetable	*horaire des départs et des arrivées (m)*
bus	*l'autobus (m)*		
...station	*gare routière (f)*		
ferry	*bateau (m)*	seat	*place (f)*
...port	*port (m)*	non-smoking	*non-fumeurs*
ticket	*billet (m)*	reserved	*réservée*
...single/return	*simple/retour (f)*	taxi!	*taxi! (m)*
yes	*oui*	help!	*au secours!*
no	*non*	today	*aujourd'hui*
please	*s'il vous-plaît*	tomorrow	*demain*
thank you	*merci*	yesterday	*hier*
hello	*bonjour*	how much?	*combien?*
goodbye	*au revoir*	expensive	*cher*
goodnight	*bonsoir*	closed	*fermé*
sorry	*pardon*	open	*ouvert*

INDEX

125

INDEX

Acknowledgements

The Automobile Association would like to thank the following photographers, libraries and associations for their assistance in the preparation of this book.

DACS *Femmes a Leur Toilette*, Pablo Picasso, © Succession Picasso/DACS 1997 67; MARY EVANS PICTURE LIBRARY 10c, 14l, 14r, 35b; ROBERT HARDING PICTURE LIBRARY 1; HULTON ARCHIVE 11; PARK ASTERIX 85c; SPECTRUM COLOUR LIBRARY 122b; www.euro.ecb.int/ 119 (euro notes)

The remaining photographs are held in the Association's own library (AA WORLD TRAVEL LIBRARY) with contributions from:
P ENTICKNAP 20b, 60, 61b; P KENWARD 27t, 28, 29, 30, 33t, 34, 35t, 36t, 40tl, 41t, 43t, 44tl, 45t, 45c, 49tr, 50tl, 51tr, 52t, 53tl. 53tr, 54, 55, 57t, 58, 63t, 65t, 66t, 70tl, 73tr; E MEACHER 37c; R MOSS 83b, 122r; D NOBLE 78, 79 80tl, 80tr, 81, 83, 83t, 84t, 85t, 86t, 86b, 87t, 87c, 88/89, 89t, 91t, 90c; K PATERSON 5t, 6t, 6c, 7t, 8t, 9t, 9c, 9b, 10t, 12t, 12b, 13t, 14t, 16c, 18b, 19b, 24c, 25b, 27b, 38, 39, 40tr, 49tl, 50b, 51b, 52b, 57c, 61t, 62, 64, 65c, 66c, 71, 75t, 89c, 91b, 117t, 117b, 122t; B RIEGER 5b, 7c, 8c, 13b, 37tl, 37b, 43b, 47, 48, 63c, 84bl. 84br; A SOUTER 2, 6b, 15t, 15b, 16t, 17t, 17c, 18t, 19t, 20t, 22t, 22c, 23t, 23b, 24t, 25t, 26t, 26c, 31, 32, 33c, 36b, 41c, 42, 44tr, 46, 50c, 51tl, 56, 59, 65b, 67, 68, 69, 70b, 72, 74, 76/77, 91t, 92/116; J A TIMS 21, 75b; W VOYSEY 17b, 70tc
Abbreviations for the above – (t) top; (b) bottom; (c) centre; (l) left; (r) right

Author's Acknowledgements

The author would like to thank Mairie de Paris, Office de Tourisme de Paris, and Comité Régional du Tourisme d'Ile de France.

Contributors
Updated by Elisabeth Morris Copy editor: Sheila Hawkins
Page Layout: Design 23 Indexer: Marie Lorimer

Dear Essential Traveller

**Your comments, opinions and recommendations are very
important to us. So please help us to improve our travel
guides by taking a few minutes to complete this simple
questionnaire.**

*You do not need a stamp (unless posted outside the UK). If you do not want to cut this page
from your guide, then photocopy it or write your answers on a plain sheet of paper.*

Send to: **The Editor, AA World Travel Guides,
FREEPOST SCE 4598, Basingstoke RG21 4GY.**

Your recommendations...

We always encourage readers' recommendations for restaurants, nightlife
or shopping – if your recommendation is used in the next edition of the
guide, we will send you a *FREE* **AA** *Essential* **Guide** of your choice.
Please state below the establishment name, location and your reasons
for recommending it.

_____

_____

_____

_____

Please send me **AA** *Essential* _____

About this guide...

Which title did you buy?
    AA *Essential* _____
Where did you buy it? _____
When? m m / y y

Why did you choose an AA *Essential* Guide? _____

_____

_____

_____

_____

Did this guide meet your expectations?
    Exceeded ☐   Met all ☐   Met most ☐   Fell below ☐
    Please give your reasons _____

_____

_____

_____

continued on next page...

Were there any aspects of this guide that you particularly liked? _____

_____

_____

Is there anything we could have done better? _____

_____

_____

About you...

Name (*Mr/Mrs/Ms*) _____

Address _____

_____

_____ Postcode _____

Daytime tel nos _____

Please only give us your mobile phone number if you wish to hear from us
about other products and services from the AA and partners by text or mms.

Which age group are you in?
Under 25 ☐ 25–34 ☐ 35–44 ☐ 45–54 ☐ 55–64 ☐ 65+ ☐

How many trips do you make a year?
Less than one ☐   One ☐   Two ☐   Three or more ☐

Are you an AA member? Yes ☐   No ☐

About your trip...

When did you book? m m / y y   When did you travel? m m / y y
How long did you stay? _____
Was it for business or leisure? _____
Did you buy any other travel guides for your trip?
If yes, which ones? _____

Thank you for taking the time to complete this questionnaire. Please send it to us as soon as
possible, and remember, you do not need a stamp (*unless posted outside the UK*).

Happy Holidays!

The Atlas

Acknowledgements
All pictures are from AA World Travel Library with contributions from the following photographers:
Bertrand Rieger: Paris by night
Clive Sawyer: street stall, Montparnasse Cemetery
Tony Souter: abstract sculpture by Centre Georges Pompidou, Moulin Rouge, neon signs

www.theAA.com
The Automobile Association's website offers comprehensive and up-to-the-minute information covering AA-approved hotels, guest houses and B&Bs, restaurants and pubs in the UK; airport parking, insurance, European breakdown cover, European motoring advice, a ferry planner, European route planner, overseas fuel prices, a bookshop and much more.

www.aaa.com
AAA's website offers comprehensive information covering AAA-approved hotels and restaurants in the US. In addition, AAA can assist US citizens with obtaining a passport, reservations and tickets for cruise, tour, motorcoach, rail and air travel. AAA provides information on independent or escorted tours for individuals or groups and offers benefits on cruises, tours and travel packages.

The Foreign and Commonwealth Office
Country advice, traveller's tips, before-
you-go information, checklists and more.
www.fco.gov.uk

French Government Tourist Office
www.franceguide.com

GENERAL
UK Passport Service
www.ukpa.gov.uk

US passport information
www.travel.state.gov

BBC – Holiday
www.bbc.co.uk/holiday

The Full Universal Currency Converter
www.xe.com/ucc/full.shtml

Flying with Kids
www.flyingwithkids.com

www.thingstodo-paris.com
www.discover-paris.info
www.paris-tourist-information.co.uk

TRAVEL
Rail and flights
www.eurostar.com
www.railbookers.com
www.raileurope.com
www.cheapflights.co.uk
www.thisistravel.co.uk
www.ba.com
www.continental.com
www.worldairportguide.com

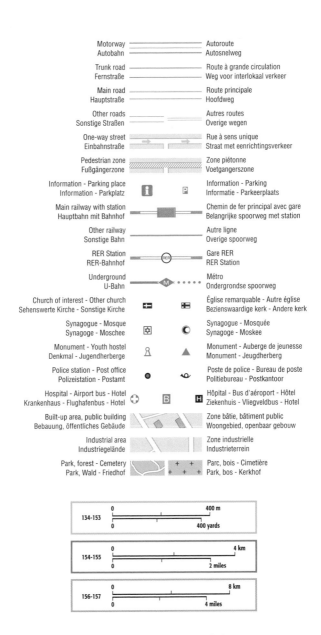

Motorway / Autobahn	Autoroute / Autosnelweg
Trunk road / Fernstraße	Route à grande circulation / Weg voor interlokaal verkeer
Main road / Hauptstraße	Route principale / Hoofdweg
Other roads / Sonstige Straßen	Autres routes / Overige wegen
One-way street / Einbahnstraße	Rue à sens unique / Straat met eenrichtingsverkeer
Pedestrian zone / Fußgängerzone	Zone piétonne / Voetgangerszone
Information - Parking place / Information - Parkplatz	Information - Parking / Informatie - Parkeerplaats
Main railway with station / Hauptbahn mit Bahnhof	Chemin de fer principal avec gare / Belangrijke spoorweg met station
Other railway / Sonstige Bahn	Autre ligne / Overige spoorweg
RER Station / RER-Bahnhof	Gare RER / RER Station
Underground / U-Bahn	Métro / Ondergrondse spoorweg
Church of interest - Other church / Sehenswerte Kirche - Sonstige Kirche	Église remarquable - Autre église / Bezienswaardige kerk - Andere kerk
Synagogue - Mosque / Synagoge - Moschee	Synagogue - Mosquée / Synagoge - Moskee
Monument - Youth hostel / Denkmal - Jugendherberge	Monument - Auberge de jeunesse / Monument - Jeugdherberg
Police station - Post office / Polizeistation - Postamt	Poste de police - Bureau de poste / Politiebureau - Postkantoor
Hospital - Airport bus - Hotel / Krankenhaus - Flughafenbus - Hotel	Hôpital - Bus d'aéroport - Hôtel / Ziekenhuis - Vliegveldbus - Hotel
Built-up area, public building / Bebauung, öffentliches Gebäude	Zone bâtie, bâtiment public / Woongebied, openbaar gebouw
Industrial area / Industriegelände	Zone industrielle / Industrieterrein
Park, forest - Cemetery / Park, Wald - Friedhof	Parc, bois - Cimetière / Park, bos - Kerkhof

134-153
0 — 400 m
0 — 400 yards

154-155
0 — 4 km
0 — 2 miles

156-157
0 — 8 km
0 — 4 miles

Maps © Mairs Geographischer Verlag / Falk Verlag, 73751 Ostfildern

St. Denis
Parc
de
Bécon
Musée
Roybet
Fould
J. B.
Joffre
E
Pont
de
Levallois
Quai Michelet
Pl. G.
Pompidou
D1
F
Square
L. Jamin
Rue
1
Maréchal
Rucher de
Levallois
Clément
Bayard
Quai
du
Musée
de la Pêche
Michelet
Rue
Pont de
Levallois-
Bécon
Baudin
Rue
Quai Vital Bouhot
Boulevard
All.
Cl. Monet
Av. G.
Pompidou
Rue
Lycée
Technique
Léonard
de Vinci
R. M. J. Bassot
Rue
R. M. Girault
Vaillant
Grande
Jatte
Boulevard Georges Seurat
Rue
Sq.
Malraux
Ernest
Rue A.
Malraux
Av. A.
Malraux
Pal. d. Sports
M. Cerdan
Parc de la
Planchette
2
Quai
Boulevard
Saussaye
Rue
R.
Pasquier
R. Jean Gabin
Grenelle
Danton
Cogniacq
Paul
Rue
LEVALLOIS
PERRET
Rue
Rue
Hôpital
Américain
V. de
Villiers
Château
Pl. de la
Libération
Rue
Kléber
Anatole
P
R.
Ma
Po
de la
St
Jacques
Clin. St.
Isabelle
Victor
Cl
Rue St. Paul
de
Hôpital N.D.
du Perpétuel
Secours
Rue
Marius
Anatole
France
M
Ca
St
Édouard
B. d
NEUILLY-SUR-
SEINE
Rue
Nortier
Chauveau
Cornby
Rue de Lesseps
Pl. du Duc
d' Orléans
Hôpital
Franco-Britann.
R. Barbès
Chaptal
Rue
R. C.
Rue
Desmoulins
3
Pa
de
Rue
Av.
Céline
Rue
Pauline
Boulevard
d'Inkermann
Bineau
Hugo
de Rouvray
Lycée
Espagnol
Villiers
Rue
Veignaud
Rue
Louise
Chapta
Rue
4
Argenson
B. d
Sq.
Belœil
Lyc.
Pasteur
Perronet
Retraite
Galighan
École
Clin. A.
Paré
Borghèse
B. d
B. d Victor Hugo
Clin.
H.Hartman
R. des Dames
Augustines
Parmentier
Bineau
B. de Duca
Villes de la P. de Vill
Av
P
v.
Ste Foy
Rue
Rue
Mairie
J. Mermoz
St-Pierre
École
Pl. W.
Churchill
Rue
R. du Gal
Cordonnier
Av. Ph. Le
Boucher
V. du Roule
Perronet
R. C. del
R. P.
Cherest
Stade
Paul
Faber
Av. de la P. de Vill
B. de
Dixmude
P
Peretti
R. de
l'Hôtel de Ville
R. St-Pierre
Rue
L. Philippe
Av.
Madeleine Michelis
du
R.
Dumas
R. Verier
R. de
l'École
de Mars
Centre
Chirurg.
P. Cherest
Pl. du G.al
Cherest
Montrosier
R. C.
Av. des Paladins
Pl. du G.al
Koenig
Pte
de Villie
P
Gouvion
Kuhn
R. de Ville
Aïcelle
d'Orléans
de
Les Sablons
M
Rue des Sablons
Pl. du
Marché
Rue de
Dulud
Sablonville
R. de Charles
R. du Midi
Pershing
Porte
des Ternes
Palais des
Congrès
Boulevard
6
ques
Charles
B. d
des Sablons
B. d
Gaulle
Laffitte
Pl. de
Verdun
RER
Porte Maillot
Pl. de la
Neuilly-
Pte-Maillot
Boulev
Barrès
Porte des
Sablons
Carrefour
des Sablons
B. d
Petit
D Maillot
B. d A.
Maurois
P. te Maillot
M
Porte
Maillot
Av.
Grande
l des Arts
Populaires
tma Gandhi
Bois de
Boulogne
Route de la Porte des Sablons à la Porte Maillot
Tramway
Square
A. et R.
Parodi
P
135
Pavillon
d'Armenonville
Mare
d'Armenon

CLICHY

WAGRAM

137

Porte de La Villette

D · E · F

Bollaert

Pl. A. Baron

Rue Magenta

Rue Davoust

Rue du

Pl. de la Gare
Marchandise

Gare Routière
Internationale

Av. de la
Pte de la V.

Chemin de Fer

Macdonald

Quai

Quai

R. de la
Clô-
L.P. Techn.
du Cirque

R. du Débar-
cadère

ture

Bd.

Rue
Danton

Station

Vaillant

Edouard

Porte de
La Villette

Cambrai

Av.

Corentin Cariou

Corentin
Cariou

St. Denis

Place du
Parvis

Cité des Sciences
et de l'Industrie

Parc

Galerie

Macdonald

Canal

R. Rouvet

de la

Argonaute

Zénith

Charente

de la

Galerie de l'Ourcq

l'Ourcq

Route des
Ponts

Maison
de Qua

Stade
Jules
Ladoumègue

Flandre

R. de

Rue de Barbanegre

R. de Nantes

l'Argonne

Gironde

Allée du Belvédère

Villette

Av. du Zénith

Bd.

ETTE

de

l'Oise

de la

Marne

Pl. du Rd.
Pt. des
Canaux

Grande
Halle

Rue

de la

Lycée

Thionville

des

Ardennes

Cité Administratives

Av. des

Porte de
Pantin

Sérurier

Rue des

P.te de
Pantin

Joinville

Quai

Quai

R. de la Meurthe

P.te de
Thionville

R. Léon Giraud

Edgar
Varèse

Conservat. de
Paris

Théâtre
Paris-Villette
Nouveau
Conservatoire
Sq.
du
Diapason

Cité
de la
Musique

Pl. de la
Porte de Pantin

R. de
la Marseillaise

R. R. de

Andou

Meaux

Jean

Rue

Lorraine

de

R. du

R. A. Danjon

Ourcq

Rue
de
Luneville

Rue
du Hainaut

G. Thill

Petit

Sente des Dorées

Av. de la
Porte Chau

Rue

Manin

Eugène Jumin

R. du

Cim. de la
Villette

Rue
Goubet

Milhaud

des
Carrières
d'Amérique

Rue
Toulouse

Ambroise
Rendu

Av. de la

Porte
Brunet

Porte
Brunet

R. du

Mewnadier

Rue

Pl. Francis
Poulenc

Allée

Darius

Rue
de la Solidarité

R.G. Pino
R. de Lorraine

R. Prévo-
yance

Brunet

Carrel

Pl. A.
Carrel

Rue

Manin

Rue

d'Haudpoul

Rue David

R. M. Hidalgo

Gal.

Brunet

Ponge
Lyc.

Sérurier

Square de la
Butte du Chap.
Rouge

Danube

d'Angers

Bd.

Sérurier

Parc

des Buttes

Chaumont

Botzaris

Rue
du

R. de la
Liberté

R. de
l'Egalite

de

progrès

Mouzaïa

R. du

des

Buttes
Chaumont

ique
hild

Botzaris

Rue du Plateau

Réservoirs
des Buttes
Chaumont

Rue des Alouettes

R. Plassard

Rue des Annelets

Rue
de
la
Villette

R. Arthur
Rozier

R. de

Compans

Bellevue

Rue E.
Cotton

des

Lilas

R. Desvaux

St Gervais

R. du

Docteur Potain

Rue

Rue
Carducci

Rue des Solitaires

Pradier

Crimée

R. L. que

Thulié

R.A.
Thierry

Pl. des
Fêtes

Coll. G.
Bude

Bois

Lycée
Hôtelière

Fessart

des
tes

141

147

Les Arrondissements de Paris

154

SAINT-OUEN

AUBERVILLIERS

Av. Michelet
Av. de la Chapelle
Av. Victor Hugo
Av. Jean Jaurès

Porte de la Chapelle **A1**

N 14

N 301

Porte d'Aubervilliers

N 2

Porte de la Villette

Porte de Clignancourt Ney

Bd. Ney

Bd. Macdonald

PANTIN

Bd. Ornano

Rue de la Chapelle

Rue de Flandre

18
Butte Montmartre

Sacré Cœur ✝

Marcadet

N 3

Jean

Porte de Pantin

LE PRÉ-ST-GERVAIS

LES LILAS

Bd. de Rochechouart

Bd. de la Chapelle

Gare du Nord

Avenue Jean Jaurès

19
Buttes Chaumonts

Porte du Pré St-Gervais

Porte des Lilas

Av. Pasteur

Opéra 9

Rue de Châteaudun

Gare de l'Est

Enclos-St-Laurent **10**

Belleville

BAGNOLET

Opéra National

Rue La Fayette

Boulevards

Bourse **2**

Place de la République

Ménilmontant **20**

Porte de Bagnolet

A3

MONTREUIL

Pl. des Victoires

Palais Royal

Louvre

Temple **3**

Centre Pompidou

St-Ambroise

Popincourt **11**

Porte de Montreuil

Palais de Justice

Hôtel de Ville **4**

Notre-Dame

Place de la Bastille

R. d. Faubourg St-Antoine

Porte de Vincennes **N 34**

N 302

Porte de Pans

6
mbourg

Panthéon

Panthéon **5**

Opéra Bastille

Diderot

Place de la Nation

Cour de Vincennes

Lagny

Porte de St-Mandé

ST-MANDÉ

Observatoire

Gare de Lyon

Gare d'Austerlitz

Reuilly **12**

Porte Dorée

Bois de Vincennes

Place d'Italie

Palais Omnisports de Paris-Bercy

Porte de Charenton

Gobelins **13**

Rue de Tolbiac

Porte de Bercy

N 6

ST-MAURICE

A6a **A6b**

N 7

Porte de Gentilly

Porte d'Italie **N 305**

Quai d'Ivry

CHARENTON

N 19

Quai des

A4

Marne

GENTILLY

LE KREMLIN-BICÊTRE

IVRY-SUR-SEINE

Pont d'Ivry

N 6

RCUEIL

155

ALFORTVILLE

Paris Street Index

A

Abbé-Carton, rue de l' 149E6–F6
Abbesses, rue des 138C4
Achille-Peretti, avenue 134C4–C5
Adolphe-Chérioux, place et square 148C3–C4
Albert-Bartholomé, avenue 148B6–C6
Albert-de-Mun, avenue 142B4
Albert-Kahn, place 139D2
Albert-1er, cours 143D3-E3
Alésia, rue d' 149E5-150A6
Alexandre-Dumas, rue 147E6–F6
Alexandre-III, pont 143E4
Alibert, rue 146B2
Aligre, place d' 152C1
Alleray, place d' 149D4
Alma, pont de l' 142C4
Alma, rue de l' 134A2–B2
Alpes, place des 152C4
Alphonse-Deville, place 150B1
Alsace, rue d' 139F6
Amiral-de-Grasse, place 142C3
Ampère, rue 136C4–D4
Amsterdam, rue d' 138B5–B6
Anatole-France, quai 144A4–B5
Anatole-France, rue 135E2–136A3
Anatole-France, rue 137D1
André-Bréchet, rue 138A1–B1
André-Honnorat, place 150C2
Anjou, quai d' 151F1
Aqueduc, rue de l' 140A5
Arago, boulevard 150C5–151E4
Arcade, rue de l' 144A1–A2
Archereau, rue 140B3–C2
Arcole, pont d' 145E6
Ardennes, rue des 141D3–E4
Argenson, boulevard d' 134C3–D4
Aristide-Briand, boulevard 134B1–C1
Aristide-Briand, rue 135F3–136C2
Armand-Carrel, rue 140C5–D5
Arnault-Tzanck, place 137F1
Arrivée, rue de l' 150A3
Arts, pont des 144C5
Assas, rue d' 150B1–C3
Auber, rue 144B1–B2
Aubervilliers, rue d' 140A4–B3
Aubreuvoir, rue de l' 134B3
Auguste-Baron, place 141E1
Auguste-Blanqui, boulevard 151D6–E6
Auguste-Vacquerie, rue 142B2–C2
Aurelle de Paladines, boulevard d' 135F5
Austerlitz, pont d' 152A3–B2
Austerlitz, quai d' 152B3–C4

B

Bac, rue du 144A6–B5
Bachaumont, rue 145D3
Bagnolet, rue de 147F5
Barbanègre, rue 141D2–D3
Barbès, boulevard 139E3–E4
Bargue, rue 149D3–E4
Bassano, rue de 142C2–C3

Bastille, boulevard de la 152B1–B2
Bastille, place de la 146B6
Bataille-de-Stalingrad, place de la 140B5
Batignolles, boulevard des 137D5–138A5
Baudin, rue 135E2–136B1
Bayard, rue 143D3
Beaubourg, rue 145E5–F3
Beaujon, rue 142C1
Beaumarchais, boulevard 146B5–B6
Beauvau, place 143F2
Bel-Air, avenue du 153F2
Bellechasse, rue de 144A4–A6
Belleville, boulevard de 146C2–147D3
Belleville, rue de 146C2–147F1
Bellevue, rue de 141E6–F6
Belliard, rue 138B2–139D1
Benjamin-Franklin, rue 142A4–A5
Bercy, boulevard de 152C4–153E4
Bercy, pont de 152C4
Bercy, quai de 152C4–153E6
Bercy, rue de 152B2–153D4
Berger, rue 145D4–E4
Berri, rue de 143D1–D2
Berthier, boulevard 136C4–137E2
Berthollet, rue 151D4
Beslay, passage 146C4
Bessières, boulevard 137E2–138A1
Béthune, quai de 151F1
Bezons, rue de 134A1–A2
Bineau, boulevard 135D3–F4
Bir-Hakeim, pont de 142A5–B6
Blanche, place 138B5
Blomet, rue 148B4–149D3
Bobillot, rue 151E6–F6
Bois, rue des 141F6
Bois-de-Boulogne, rue du 134B5
Bois-le-Prêtre, boulevard du 138A1
Boissière, rue 142A2–B3
Bolnod, rue 139E2–E3
Bonaparte, rue 144C5–150B1
Bonne-Nouvelle, boulevard de 145E2
Bosquet, avenue 143D4–D6
Botzaris, rue 141D6
Boucry, rue 140A2
Boulets, rue des 153E1
Bourbon, quai de 145F6
Bourdon, boulevard 152B1–B2
Bourdonnais, rue des 145D4–D5
Bourgogne, rue de 143F5
Boyer, rue 147E2–E3
Brancion, rue 148C6–149D5
Branly, quai 142B6–C4
Bréguet-Sabin, square 146B5
Brésil, place du 137D4
Bretagne, rue de 146A4
Breteuil, avenue de 149E1–E2
Breteuil, place de 149E2
Broca, rue 151D5–E4
Brun, rue le 151E5–F4
Budapest, place de 138B6

C

Cambrai, rue de 140C2–141D2
Cambronne, place 148C2
Cambronne, rue 148C2–149D3
Campagne-Première, rue 150B4
Capucines, boulevard des 144B2–C2
Cardinet, rue 137D5–F3
Carnot, avenue 142B1
Carnot, rue 136A2–B3
Carrousel, place du 144B4–C4
Carrousel, pont du 144B5
Castiglione, rue de 144B3
Catalogne, place de 149F4
Caulaincourt, rue 138B4–139D3
Cavendish, rue 140C5–141D5
Célestins, quai des 145F6
Chaligny, rue 153D1–D2
Championnet, rue 138B2–139E2
Champs-Élysées, avenue des 142C2–143F3
Champs-Élysées, rond point des 143E2
Chance-Milly, rue 137D1–D2
Change, pont au 145D5
Chanzy, rue 147D6–E6
Chapelle, boulevard de la 139E5–140A4
Chapelle, place de la '139F4
Chapelle, rue de la 140A1–A3
Charenton, rue de 153E3–F5
Charles-de-Gaulle, avenue 134B4–135E6
Charles-de-Gaulle, place 134A2–B2
Charles-de-Gaulle, place 142B1–C1
Charles-Floquet, avenue 142B5–C6
Charles-Hermite, rue 140A1–B1
Charles-Laffitte, rue 134C5–135E6
Charles-Michels, place 148A2
Charles-Risler, avenue 142C6
Charolais, rue du 153D3–E4
Charonne, boulevard de 147E5–153F1
Charonne, rue de 146C6–147F5
Chartran, rue 134C4
Château, boulevard du 134C4–135E2
Château, rue du 134C4
Château-du-Loir, avenue de 134A1–B1
Châteaudun, rue de 144B1–D1
Château-Landon, rue du 140A5–A6
Châtelet, place du 145D5
Chaussée-d'Antin, rue de la 144B1–C2
Chauveau, rue 135D2–E3
Chemin-Vert, rue du 146B5–147E4
Cherche-Midi, rue du 149F2–150B1
Chevalier de la Barre, rue du 139D4
Chevert, rue 143D6–E5
Chézy, rue de 135D4–E3
Choisy, avenue de 151F6
Circulaire, boulevard 134A3
Cité, rue de la 145D6–E6
Claude-Bernard, rue 151D3–E4
Claude-Debussy, rue 136B4
Claude-Vellefaux, avenue 146B1–B2